Can the Dead
Communicate
with the Living?

I. M. HALDEMAN

Can the Dead Communicate with the Living?

BAKER BOOK HOUSE
Grand Rapids, Michigan

Paperback edition issued 1976
by Baker Book House

ISBN: 0-8010-4141-4

PRINTED BY DICKINSON BROTHERS, INC.
GRAND RAPIDS, MICHIGAN
1976

Contents

6 Contents

I

THE DEAD

THE indescribable war through whose aftermath the world is now passing has left as its memorial a holocaust of slain.

Ten millions of earth's flower of young manhood sleep beneath the poppies of Flanders' field, beneath the lilies of France, the fair, blue skies of Italy, the burning sands of Syrian deserts and beneath the snows of Russia—husbands, fathers, sons, brothers, friends and sweethearts.

And the living will not let them go.

They cannot believe them dead.

They did not go as the dead go—with closed eyes and still hands and feet that tread no path.

They went out from the midst, leaving the memory of the virile, yet tender caress, the brave smile that rebuked a tear and the high courage that confronted a sacrifice.

They did not die as others die.

They did not languish upon beds of pain, of slow wasting sickness and the sullen fires of unchecked fever.

Faces of the loved ones did not look upon them, tender hands from home did not soothe them.

They went as when the mower's scythe cuts down the ripening grain; as when rude hands snatch the rose from the flowering bush; as when a star slips from the galaxies of the night, leaving only the void of darkness; as when the sun goes down at noon; as when the song in its loftiest lilt quivers, breaks, the refrain is hushed and there is only the chorus of choking sobs and the rain of tears.

And the living will not let them go.

The father still dreams of the plans he had made when the son of his pride should win the coveted place and be to him as a bulwark, a refuge, a retreat, a consolation in the deepening shadows of his declining years.

The mother still listens for the rushing sound of boyish footsteps and the old familiar cry, " Hello! Mother! " entwining in the lusty accents some pet and loving name.

The sister through blinding tears keeps dear memory of the brawny strength of a comrade brother ever at her side to kid and help her.

The wife staggers and is near to swoon as she waits in vain for the strong arms that once framed her against a throbbing heart, and the whispered words of loyal love that thrilled and filled her.

Children look up with a strange wistfulness and wide eyes of painful wonder and cannot understand why Father comes no more.

The living will not let them go.

They will not let them pass beyond.

Nay! they stretch out their hands and fain would so hold them that they may not pass a moment from life's daily ways and ken. Yea, they make them halt and step out of the unwonted procession always gliding to the night, the night that never turns to morning.

And Memory comes to reign and rule and take on strength and vividness and all commanding power that makes the past return.

The living live over again the companionship of their dead. They walk or ride or drive with them the old roads, the fields, the woodlands and the oft frequented paths. They take up the old letters, almost faded, some of them, write them over, typewrite them. They read into them or out of them a concept of character, splendid bravery and manly worth such as they never dreamed were in these dear and absent lives. They take up a book at a page turned down, and refuse to read beyond. They sit in the room that was specially theirs and breathe in the lingering atmosphere of sad, of bitter, yet sweetest yesterdays. They collect the pictures of the dear ones, dearest to them now, and arrange them on desk or wall, gaze on them till the eyes in the picture seem to move and the lips, wreathed with the old smile, almost open and the gazer waits spellbound, thinking to hear them speak again.

No! the living will not let them go.

They reach out and hold them with an intensity such as in no hour did the living ever reach out and claim their dead.

Never since the world began did the living ever ask such questions concerning their dead as they are asking to-day; and never such determination to break down all partitions between the absent somewhat, whatever it may be that personalized those bodies so silent, but once so vibrant, so responsive to the thought of those who loved them.

The intensity and the longing are so great that though there be little noise or outcry, yet never was the world so conscious of the tragedy and the heart ache that is uttered in the simple and most common phrase:

" He is dead."

The living are asking three straight questions:

" Where are they? "

" What are they? "

" Are they? "

And the response to these questions is coming.

It is coming in a literature as thick as wind-blown leaves of Autumn.

And strangest of winds blowing them in heaps to fill the counters and the shelves of book shops. Friends are loaning books about the dead to one another. They are reading them in cars, in the homes, everywhere, everybody is reading this sudden, wide-spreading literature.

The response is coming.

It is coming in a thronging crowd of mediums, in mediumistic séances, tilting of tables, in script communications, in planchette redivivus—in the ouija board.

All classes are engaged in these things, the high, the low, the rich, the poor, the uncultured and the cultured, the ignorant and the learned, men of thought, of science and philosophy—representative men, men whose very names win attention.

The questions are coming from all over the world.

Many have been coming to me by letters and by personal inquiry.

I shall answer these questions.

I shall set forth what Holy Scripture testifies concerning the unseen world of the dead, the purported communications therefrom, the present state of the dead and their future.

II

SCRIPTURE TEACHES A CERTAIN CLASS OF THE DEAD DO COME BACK, ENTER IN AND POSSESS THE BODIES OF THE LIVING

THESE are called "devils," but the word should be "demons"; as it is written:

"Now the Spirit speaketh expressly, that in the latter times some shall depart from the faith, giving heed to seducing (wandering) spirits, and doctrines of devils (demons)" (1 Timothy 4: 1).

That demons are the souls of persons who once lived on this earth is demonstrated by one of the most dramatic scenes in the New Testament, the story of the demoniac of Gadara, as related in the Gospel according to Saint Luke.

Our Lord had sailed across the Sea of Galilee. He landed on the shore of Gadara. Immediately a man came running down the hillside. He was covered with rags and tatters. Broken chains hung from his wrists and rattled from his ankles as he ran. His hair was disheveled, his face pale as the face of the dead, his eyes like flaming wells of fire. He fell down at the feet of the Lord and in a raucous voice cried out:

"What have I to do with thee, Jesus, thou Son of God most high? I beseech thee, torment me not."

"What is thy name?" inquired the Lord.

He answered:

"Legion; for we are many."

The spirit who was spokesman for the rest besought Him that He would not cast them out into the deep.

They asked Him to let them go into the two thousand swine feeding on the heights.

He gave them permission. They entered the swine and the whole herd ran violently down and were choked in the sea.

The word "deep" is the key that demonstrates and explains the identity of the spirits.

To the average reader, because of the proximity of the scene to the lake, the conclusion would be that it was the lake that was meant by the word "deep."

A moment's consideration will show this could not be.

Spirits are immaterial, impalpable things. They could have no fear of water. The lake could produce no effect upon them.

The word "deep" is "abyss."

"Abyss" in the New Testament signifies "hades."

Hades of the New Testament is "sheol," of the Old.

Sheol or hades is the abode of the disembodied souls of those who once lived on earth.

Before the resurrection of our Lord Jesus Christ all the disembodied dead went thither, the righteous and the unrighteous.

The unrighteous went into a portion belonging to them.

The righteous went into another separated from it by a fixed gulf and known in our Lord's day as "Abraham's Bosom."

That this is no mere Jewish legend or ornamentation of perfervid and undisciplined imagination is demonstrated in the story (by no sane exegesis can it be called a parable) of the Rich Man and Lazarus.

The Rich Man is seen in that part of hades which he himself styles as " this place of torment "; while Lazarus and Abraham are visible across the " fixed " gulf in the location called by our Lord Himself—"Abraham's Bosom."

Shortly before He died our Lord announced He would be three days and three nights in the heart of the earth.

" The heart of the earth " is equivalent to " abyss," " bottomless pit," and signifies " hades," the unseen world of the dead.

Just before He died He said to the repentant thief (whom with His nailed hands He snatched from the depths of perdition) " To-day shalt thou be with me in paradise."

As by His announcement that He would be three days and three nights in the heart of the earth He affirmed He would descend into hades; as hades is the abode of the disembodied dead, then when He died He did descend into hades; and as He promised the thief should go with Him that day, then that day both He and the thief descended into hades; as the holy and sinless Son of God could not go into that portion called "this place of torment," He did go into the abode reserved for the righteous, into that part called "Abraham's Bosom," and took the thief whom He had pardoned with Him.

On the third day He rose from the dead and, according to Saint Paul in the fourth of Ephesians, took up with Him the souls of the righteous dead, including the thief, and took them *unto* the third heaven and then *into* paradise, and finally into the New Jerusalem, the place He went to prepare.

Since that day the dead who die in the Lord depart to be with Christ in Heaven; wherefore it is written:

"Absent from our home, *out of the body,* and immediately present at *our home—with the Lord.*"

Only the Christless dead now descend into hades. They descend where the Rich Man was seen, into the "place of torment."

As the spirits who infested the man of Gadara plead that they might not be sent into the "deep"; as the deep is hades; and as only the souls of those who once lived on earth and died could go there, then these demons were the disembodied souls of human beings; and as they were disembodied spirits, then they had already been in hades and were pleading with the Lord that He would not send them back.

III

ONLY A SPECIAL CLASS OF THE CHRISTLESS DEAD COME BACK

THEY are called "unclean" spirits, "wicked" spirits.

They are the vile, unspeakably vicious, monstrous and outbreaking sinners of the earth.

The Son of God gives a description of some of them.

He says:

"When the unclean spirit is gone out of a man, he walketh through dry places (literally, "waterless place," that is, "hades," where the rich man could not find a drop of water; the place of which Zechariah, the prophet, speaks as, "the pit without water") seeking rest, and findeth none,

"Then he saith, I will return into my house from whence I came out; and when he is come, he findeth it empty, swept and garnished.

"Then goeth he, and taketh with himself seven other spirits more wicked than himself, and they enter in and dwell there: and the last state of that man is worse than the first."

While it is true the "unclean" spirit is the spirit of idolatry, nevertheless, the Apostle Paul tells us the sacrifice that is offered to idols is in reality offered to " demons "; while it is true our Lord is forecasting the hour when the Jewish nation after the translation of the Church shall fall down and worship the image set up by Anti-Christ (as of old that of the Roman Emperor was set up) yet is he giving the description of an actual fact and corroborates the statement that the wicked dead can come out of hades, enter in and dwell in the bodies of men as their houses.

They break out of hades as prisoners break out of jail.

They are jail breakers.

And just as jail breakers are in collusion with those outside they find the Devil outside (he is not in hades and will not be till the beginning of the thousand years, the millennium) and obtain from him all the aid they need.

They bring no revelation from hades.

They attempt no description of the world of the dead.

They have but one purpose in coming forth.

They seek to incarnate themselves.

They seek bodies as the instrument to carry out their own sinful, infamous and filthy desires. They seek naturally the bodies of those who have cultivated the sins and moral diseases akin to their own.

The effect upon the bodies of those whom they possess is disastrous.

They ruin the mind.

They ruin health and happiness.

Many of the diseases which the most scientific diagnostician cannot determine, and the most skilful practitioner cannot cure, may be accounted for by demon possession as in the days of the Lord.

And it is to be remembered that He performed his mightiest cures by casting the demons out of the afflicted as the efficient cause of all their trouble.

In very significant language we are told:

" He went about doing good (mark what kind of good) healing all that were oppressed (under the power) of the Devil."

According to the word of prophecy just before the Coming of the Son of God to this world again the pit will be widely opened and, as a spiritualist once expressed it: " they will come a great horde " in riotous invasion, running, flying, leaping, cursing until the very heart of men shall be submerged and hopelessly polluted by the " ghostly canaille." They will so come tumultuously and insanely frollicking and full of the deviltry of their malicious filthiness and unspeakable iniquity; they will so thoroughly seize and possess men and use every faculty and organ for themselves to gratify their own desires that for a prophesied five months men driven mad, wholly beside themselves will seek death; but death, we are told, will flee from them; they will be baffled and held in life by their tormentors in their determination not to go back to the pit from which they come; they will so control them that none during that agonizing period of desire for suicide will be able to accomplish his attempt.

"And he opened the bottomless pit (hades) ; and there arose a smoke out of the pit, as the smoke of a great furnace (the rich man in hades said, ' I am tormented in this flame ') ; and the sun and the air were darkened by reason of the smoke of the pit.

"And there came out of the smoke locusts (demons) upon the earth: and unto them was given power, as the scorpions of the earth have power."

They were commanded to hurt only those men which should not have the seal of God in their foreheads.

"And to them it was given that they should not kill them, but that they should be tormented five months. . . .

"And in those days shall men seek death, and shall not find it; and shall desire to die, and death shall flee from them " (Revelation 9: 2–6).

IV

SCRIPTURE TEACHES GOD ONCE PERMITTED A PROPHET TO COME BACK FROM THE DEAD AND TALK WITH A KING OF ISRAEL

THAT prophet was Samuel.

The king was Saul.

The conditions and circumstances in Saul's case were intense.

Samuel was dead.

Saul had gone from bad to worse.

He had fallen down from his plane of splendid possibilities as a king. He had been swallowed up in his madness of jealousy, envy and ambition. He had yielded his soul to hatred and its final outcome of murder in intent and attempt. He had turned from the Lord. He no longer sought the mind and will of God in His Word. He had leaned to his own understanding and had followed his own will, sought only to satisfy his own desires. The Lord had turned from him and had given him up to his own way and the disasters he was logically bringing upon his own head. He was surrounded by enemies. The Philistines were marshalling their hosts against him. He was at his wit's end.

He looked upon the coming morrows and the impending conflict with a mind and heart thoroughly disintegrated.   He was filled with fear and despair. The priests could give him no wisdom.   He could get no response, neither by Urim nor Thummim. He thought involuntarily of Samuel.   Samuel it is true again and again had hewed him with the Word of the Lord and had been the messenger of the Lord's judgment against him; nevertheless, he fain would hear from him as of old.   If he were alive he would go to him and seek his counsel. Why not seek it now?   Samuel was, indeed, dead; but there were those who had the power, it was said, to bring the dead up from hades and compel them to speak.   Then he remembered he had but lately sent out an edict against all who had familiar spirits, an edict which called for death of medium, wizard or necromancer; but, it was possible the law had not been carried out strictly.

No sooner was the idea in his mind than it held him.

He made known his desire to some of the intimates of his court.

There were two who knew of a woman who had a familiar spirit, a trance medium.   She lived amid the rocks at Endor.

He determined to go see her and use her powers.

He had fallen very low.

He was making himself a willing instrument not only to violate the law of God, but to violate his own promulgation of that law and in trampling on his own edict to trample on his own dignity and honour as king and guardian of the laws. He was willing to shame himself before the men over whom he should maintain himself in righteousness and faithfulness.

He disguised himself.

He took his two intimates with him.

They mounted their horses and rode toward Endor.

They rode on in the night.

They rode to Endor.

The king forced his horse up the rocky defile to the cave where the woman dwelt.

Ears that were alert would have heard the hoofs of the king's horse ring out on the startled night.

The streams from the upper ridges plashed and gurgled like voices that whispered and laughed.

The winds were astir and full of moanings.

The low hung branches of the sparse trees swept the king's face as he bent low to the ears of his horse's head as though, like clutching hands, they would hold him back.

The stars gleamed out from the night like watching and sorrowful eyes.

They reached the cave. A light shone through the crevice of the rude door.

They knocked.

The door was opened and the woman shrank back.

The king bent from his great height and told her his errand.   He had come that she might bring up from the dead him whom he should name to her.

She protested.

Did they not know Saul, the king, had lately sent out an edict ordering all who had familiar spirits to be put to death? She was sure they had come to spy her out and put her life in jeopardy. She was not willing to have aught to do with them. She would not lend herself to her own destruction.

Then the king swore by the Lord God that no harm should befall her.

Thus he swore, he who had broken the law of God and was now violating his own edict, that he would keep faith with her.   He swore should she yield to his request she should be safe.

Then she asked him whom she should bring up?

He bade her bring up Samuel, the prophet.

The woman was a medium with the " control " of a familiar spirit.   She expected to go into a trance and then the spirit making use of her organs of speech, but simulating them as from the depths of the earth like a ventriloquist, would personate Samuel and fool Saul.

Suddenly the woman gave a shriek.

All unexpectedly to her and her " control " she saw a spirit rising like a wraith from the earth, becoming fixed and standing there as an accusing thing, dreadful and terrible in its very silence and mystery.   She was overcome with horror. She had played her game of deception a long while. She had had intercourse with the familiar spirit and knew the power of such; but this was a reality out of the realm of the dead. With shivering fear and in accents of terror she turned to Saul, crying out:

"Why hast thou deceived me? for thou art Saul."

The king bade her not to be afraid, but tell him what she saw.

She told him she saw gods ascending out of the earth.

To her terrified vision they were many.

All intent upon his own idea, thinking only of one person, of Samuel alone, the king inquired of the woman what form he was.

She answered that she saw an old man coming up and he was covered with a mantle.

Then we are told Saul himself perceived it was Samuel and stooping down low before him listened to the voice that came from him.

From that moment, according to the divine record, all the conversation is between Saul and Samuel. The woman has no relation to it. She becomes a mere side figure in the scene.

Samuel actually came back and was materialized.

It was an amazing spectacle.

That wraith in the dimness and shadows of the cave, the flickering light of the lamp only making the obscurity and mystery more intense, and Saul bowed, shivering and listening to the solemn words of his doom.

Samuel asks him why, since the Lord has turned away from him and he has himself acknowledged it, why has he come to seek wisdom from the dead; why will he listen to him dead whom he so wilfully resisted when alive? He tells him his present state is as he had been forewarned; tells him the kingdom has been rent from him and given to that David against whom he had sought to act so murderously, that his army should be defeated, put to flight, and he and his sons be slain.

When Saul heard that he fell all his length on the floor of the cave. So sore was his state the woman was moved with compassion for him and, setting food before him, insisted he should eat.

He took a little and then with his companions rode away into the fateful night.

No revelation did Samuel give concerning himself and the state of those in the underworld of the dead. He says simply that he had been in a condition of quiet and rest and Saul's intrusion had disturbed him.

From Genesis to Revelation this is the only instance in Holy Scripture where God permitted the dead in Christ to come back and hold communication with the living.

Samuel came back because God sent him to verify the truth of the warnings He had previously given by the prophet and as a climacteric judgment against Saul.   He would punish him not only for the evil of his course in turning away from the Word of the Lord so plainly and specially given him through the prophet, but because he had broken the law against seeking communication from the dead, had doubly broken it in that he had transgressed his own edict and put his office as king to shame.

Therefore it was the Lord who slew him, caused him to die in the hour of battle; as it is written:

" So Saul died for his transgression which he committed against the Lord, even against the word of the Lord, which he kept not, and also for asking counsel of one that had a familiar spirit, to inquire of it.   And inquired not of the Lord; therefore he slew him, and turned the kingdom unto David, the son of Jesse."

V

THE CHRISTIAN DEAD DO NOT COME BACK; NOR DO THEY IN ANY WISE COMMUNICATE WITH THE LIVING

THIS negative proposition is sustained by presumptive, direct and corroborative evidence.

The evidence is presumptive.

For a Christian to leave Heaven and come to this world to communicate with the living through the instrumentality of a medium, that Christian would have to enter into a conspiracy with the medium to inspire the people of God to violate the law by which He forbids them to seek communication with the dead. Since the law which forbids the people of God to hold communion with the dead is equally authoritative for the people of God who have died that they should not consent to hold communion, then the Christian in Heaven who should respond to the medium or the call of any one on earth would be seeking to have the law of God broken by both the living and the dead.

Can you conceive of a Christian in Heaven, in the company of the holy prophets, the holy apostles, saints and angels of God, and in the presence of Him who has redeemed them and lifted them into the Heaven place, into that court where holiness is the fashion, where all insincerity and rebellion and all lawlessness are banished; can you conceive of such an one entering into collusion with the sinful of earth against the Lord in Heaven?

Such a proposition in the very nature of the thing is not thinkable.

If it is not thinkable, it is not debatable.

Again:

It is impossible for any soul to leave Heaven and enter into conspiracy for this double violation without the permission and exercised power of the Lord.

For such an one to leave Heaven under the mandate of the Lord would be to carry authority to any and all on earth to seek to the dead and thus testify the Lord delighted to break His own law and nullify and dishonour His own Word.

Is that thinkable?

By the wildest stretch of imagination or the surrender of most ordinary and commonplace logic it is not thinkable.

If it is not thinkable it is not open to discussion.

It may be offered as an objection that the case of Samuel is a precedent wherein the Lord violated His own law in sending him back from the dead.

The answer is, the Lord sent him not as an encouragement to men to seek unto the dead, but as a judgment against the very thing.

He slew Saul because he had entered into a conspiracy with a medium to hold communication with the dead.

The death of Saul is the most dynamic denunciation of God against those who do seek to have that communication.

The death of Saul was God's affirmation of His law against seeking to the dead and a terrific witness of God's integrity behind His law.

Samuel came back, as he had been on earth, the minister of God's judgment.

His coming back and the manner of it, together with the death and disaster that followed is a witness that his case was an exception and intended to emphasize the law of God against either the return of the dead or the seeking thereto.

The evidence is direct.

In the sixth chapter of the Revelation we learn so soon as the dead in Christ reach Heaven they are anxious to have the news of those whom they have left on earth.

It is a presumptive proposition and yet directly logical to say, had they had both permission and power to come back and see for themselves or by any means to hold communication with those on earth, both for their own sakes as a matter of comfort and to give the comfort of first hand assurance to the others, they would come at once.

The record settles the question.

So far from coming back or being permitted to come back they are told to rest—and the sense of

the word is to halt, to stay where they are; then
the angels who, in this book of the Revelation, are
the active figures of communication, tell them some
news concerning those for whom they have inquired.

" It was said unto them that they should rest."

That is, it was said unto them they should
remain where they were and be in a state of refreshment and rest.

That is evidence enough and direct enough.

The evidence is still further direct.

The dead who depart to be with Christ cannot
return till the Lord returns in the morning of the
resurrection.

This is the testimony of Job.

He says:

"All the days of my appointed time will I wait
till my change come."

He has been asking himself the question about
death.

If he dies shall he live again?

He is not raising any question about continued
existence, but, rather, whether he shall come forth
again in bodily form.

He answers his own question.

He will descend into hades. His body will become but a bundle of bones; yet he esteems this
body is the work of the Lord's hands. With the
Psalmist he looks upon himself as fearfully and
wonderfully made. The Lord will remember this

work of His hands. He will have a desire for it. He has appointed a time when He will call it forth. That time we now know is the First Resurrection at the Second Coming of our Lord. He says his Redeemer will call. Job will answer. He shall come forth and see Him face to face.

But he says:

"All the days of my appointed time I will wait."

We know when the Lord ascended He took Job along with the rest of the saints in hades to Heaven with Himself; that, therefore, now, he is to rest in Heaven till the morning without clouds.

" I will wait."

The word means—to tarry.

He will tarry where he now is till the Lord shall come again.

The Psalmist utters the same thought.

He says:

" Weeping may endure for a night, but joy cometh in the morning."

He is thinking of the morning of the resurrection.

In another psalm he expresses the effect the resurrection morning will have upon him.

He says:

"As for me I will behold thy face in righteousness. I shall be satisfied when I awake with thy likeness."

The Old Testament saints knew only of hades as their resting place till the morning; but they knew they would rest and have no further relation with the inhabitants of the earth till that great morning.   When we come to the New Testament we find Paul comforting the Thessalonian saints concerning their dead in Christ with a special revelation from the Lord.   He bids them not to sorrow as others which have no hope.   The comfort with which he comforts them is neither that they shall die and go to Heaven, nor that those who are there can come forth in their disembodied state; but that the Lord Himself is coming (and may come any time) to bring them from Heaven and their bodies from the grave, unite them, make their bodies immortal, and bring both the dead and the living together in the beauty and the glory of that triumphant morning.

This unbreakable, direct evidence is corroborated.

It is corroborated by the scene in hades between the rich man and Abraham.

The rich man pleads that Abraham will send Lazarus back to his father's house that he may warn his five brothers that they may not come into "this place of torment."

Abraham refuses.

He will not allow Lazarus to go.   He cannot leave his place of rest.

If the pleading of one who has been shut out from all hope and who is filled with evangelistic fervour, even though its objective be selfishly limited to the pleading for his own family cannot prevail; if the intensity of his realization of the awful misery into which he had fallen could not succeed in bringing Lazarus back as a witness of continued existence and as a terrific warning to the living, neither, and in the nature of the case, can the effort of any medium succeed in bringing from Heaven and its ordained, uninterrupted peace those who have entered there.

This corroborative evidence is itself corroborated and strengthened by the moral reason Abraham gives why Lazarus could not be sent back. He says the five brethren have Moses and the prophets and must hear them; that in them is the way of salvation and all the warning needed to enable them to shun the prison place of the lost.

This is simply saying the Lord God has shut the world up to the written revelation which He Himself has given.

This is in accord with what the prophet Isaiah had said:

" Should not a people seek unto their God?"

" Should the living seek unto the dead?"

Nay! there is no need.

" To the law and to the testimony."

Beyond all question then the Word of the living God teaches the Christian dead do not come back, nor do they in any manner whatsoever hold communication with, nor give communications or messages to the living.

VI

ALL PURPORTED COMMUNICATIONS
FROM THE DEAD ARE MADE
BY FALLEN ANGELS

THESE angels are divided into two classes. Those angels who in the antediluvian age left their own habitation in one of the upper worlds, came down to earth and entered in unto the daughters of men whose beauty had tempted them and begot a hybrid race called giants, or the nephilim, beings half angel, half man, the persons who are spoken of in classic literature as the demi-gods, the mighty ones who figure more or less in the lore of all nations; figure there with all the added fancies and imaginations of men, because the primal revelation given of God fell from their hands; and, as when a vase on which a portrait has been painted falls, is broken, and different hands pick up the fragments, so that each has a part, but an incomplete part of the whole, even so among the nations scattered after the flood, each had a fragment of the truth, polished and embellished to suit the desire.

The Lord caused the sinning angels to be arrested.

They were taken down as prisoners to a place of imprisonment below hades, or the very lowest part of hades called tartarus and, according to the Apostle Peter writing under the inspiration of God, shut up in dark cells, chained and held there until the final judgment day when the Lord shall settle all things.

The other fallen angels are those who took part in the rebellion of Satan.

Satan was the first being created.

He is called, " Son of the morning," " the morning star," and " Lucifer, the Light-bearer."

Speaking by the mouth of Ezekiel, the Lord says he was created perfect in all his ways.

He was full of wisdom. He was perfect in beauty. He was, next to God, supreme in power.

Because of this exalted endowment and equipment the Lord God appointed him to be prince of this earth when it was first created.

He gave him the cherubim to be associated with him in the perfect earth which He had created as a particular province in His measureless empire.

The beauty of Lucifier, his genius, his splendour, his power and his superiority to others were his ruin.

He became self-conscious and filled with audacious ambition—an ambition that fitted his greatness.

He was not willing to be a subordinate God.

He was not willing to rule the world as the vice-gerent of God.

He determined to rule the world for himself. He would be its God, independent and unhampered of God.

It was an issue of personality in respect to pre-eminence, dignity and will.

Here was the origin of sin.

All sin in its essence and consequence is rooted in one thing—the clash of any personal will with the will of God.

The will of Lucifer clashed with the will of God.

It was an assault upon the supremacy of the eternal, not in power, for there was no possibility of competition in that, the creature with the Creator—but—in will.

This clash with the will of God was high treason.

This was sin.

The sin of self-will, self-exaltation in a creature of God was the matrix out of which has come forth all other sin.

In thus exalting himself against God Lucifer became—Satan; for " satan " means, " adversary."

In justification of himself he accused the Lord (as afterward he accused Him before man). In becoming the accuser of God he became—the Devil; for " devil " signifies " accuser."

Thus Lucifer made himself Satan and Devil, adversary and accuser of the Most High God.

God made him perfect and clean. He made himself Satan.

God gave him liberty, glory and power. He made himself the Devil.

This answers the question: "Why did God make the Devil?"

He never made one.

He became one by his own act.

He rebelled against God.

The cherubim associated with him took sides with him and became rebels like himself.

God smote him and his angels.

He smote the earth which had been the scene of this rebellion.

The earth fell into a state of sheer chaos.

Jarred from its original orbit about the sun it floated in space a black, drowned, sunless, silent thing like a funeral convoy.

No record is given of how long this chaos lasted.

Six thousand years ago God withdrew it from its chaotic state, lifted it back into its full orbit, caused the sun to shine again through the encompassing darkness and reformed it as the earth of to-day.

He created man to take the place of Satan as its prince, its Lord and God.

Satan and his angels were banished to "outer darkness."

"The outer darkness" of Scripture is the zone outside of the earth's atmosphere, between it and the atmospheric enclosures of the other planets in the starry universe.

Satan was given permission to ascend from time to time to the third heaven into the presence of the Lord as the accuser of the Lord's people when they should fall by the way and fail to make confession of their faults.

He was given full liberty to range the earth.

Man was no sooner created than he tempted him with the temptation that had caused his own fall.

He suggested to him that he had all the equipment necessary to rule the world without God.

He could create a race in his own image and fill the world.

He did not need to be in leading strings to the Almighty. He had creative life power and should use it.

The office and powers of rulership that God had given to man were, however, altogether probationary. The office could be kept and the powers exercised only by an absolute dependency of faith in and upon God.

In proportion as he would walk by faith God would make him the channel of His own powers, the instrument and revelation of Himself; he should be His incarnation. He was already His constitutional image in that he was a threefold being, spirit, soul and body. It was his privilege to be His moral and spiritual image, reflecting His character of holiness and righteousness.   He could be, if he were willing to make the will of God supreme in his life, the governmental image of God, representing Him in His supreme authority, standing for Him so that He should be seen and known in man.   It was thus God's purpose to make man His visibility.

But he listened to the Devil's lie rather than to God's truth.   He set up his own will instead of the will of God.

The result was immediate and terrific.   His spirit connection with God was broken.   He slipped down into and under the control of the material and animal side of his life.   He became the enthronement of Satan and not God.

This was his fall.

Instead of becoming the enthronement of the God of the universe, he became the enthronement of the rebel of the universe.

He was not created to be an animal working with tools; but, as the enthronement of God he should have spoken and it would have been done; he should have commanded and it would have stood fast.

Since the hour of his fall he has been trying to get back to his place as the full God of the earth.

He has been protesting against his limitations.

Every invention he has made is the expression of that protest.

These inventions, in spite of himself, instead of

proclaiming his greatness announce his limitation and littleness.

Does he invent a telescope, it is because his eyesight falls short.   Does he invent a telephone, it is because his hearing is limited.   Does he congratulate himself that he can speed almost with the swiftness of the wind on his tracks of steel, it is witness that his powers of locomotion are limited. Gather up all his inventions and in every direction and they shall be seen to be the crutches with which he who might have been as a god is trying to limp his way upward to the throne of supreme power he feels in his inmost soul belongs of right to him.

His very greatness in these matters, in the making of these crutches, bear witness of his fearful lameness, of his terrible fall.

In the original charter God gave him dominion and rule over the earth and placed " all things under his feet."

Instead of that, he is to-day under the feet of all things.

All his science, his increase in knowledge and power are the mad efforts to turn the Devil's lie, " ye shall be as gods," into verified and effective truth.

By his stroke against man the Devil (still retaining his title as " prince of this world, acknowledged as such by the Son of God and declared by Paul to be the god of this world) has succeeded in keeping man as man and man's world in his power and is moving steadily forward to that hour when in imitation of God he shall incarnate himself in the man of sin, the son of perdition, fool the world with a false Christ, an imitation Christ, and for a brief period set up that kingdom, that super state whose pretentious peace and prosperity shall deceive the sons of men; and were it not for the power of God over all, for that God who makes the wrath of man to praise Him and the remainder restrains, should deceive the very elect.

Although Satan has been given the range of the earth, he has never descended into hades. He will not enter it till the Second Coming of our Lord Jesus Christ when he will be incarcerated there during the thousand years, during the millennial reign of the Son of God.

Satan's rebel angels were shut out from the heaven of heavens. They were not sent down into hades, but with their head and master given full liberty in the earth.

They are called—" wandering spirits."

They are " lying " and " wicked " spirits.

They are the rulers of the world's darkness.

They are the kosmokratores, the " cosmic powers."

They are behind the governments of the world, back of the thrones of kings, the chairs of presidents and governors, in the cabinets of the nations, mixing and muddling the politics of the world, inspiring its wars, its conflicts, lawlessnesses and confusion.

As it is written:

"We wrestle not against flesh and blood, but against principalities, against powers, against the rulers, the potentates, the cosmic powers of this darkness, against wicked spirits in the heavens."

They have great knowledge and mighty powers.

They can make themselves visible and invisible. They can materialize and dematerialize themselves.

They can come and go as the winds come and go.

They can enter the home.

They can see and yet remain unseen.

For this reason women are commanded to keep covered, that is to keep the head covered, with a vail.

As it is written:

"For this cause (on account of her constitutional relation to man) ought the woman to have a vail on her head because of the angels."

They are full of impish curiosity.

They listen, they hear.

They can hear the secrets of a family; and for this reason can, through mediums, report things known only to the individuals themselves; or, bring news known to others concerning them and in a measure predict certain events.

Many things occurring in mediumistic spheres which seem entirely supernatural and evidential have been exposed as tricks of legerdemain, as wholly fraudulent, and practised with absolute intent to deceive, as in the case of Howe caught by Browning and hated by him because of it, and the escapades of Euspasia Palladino; to say nothing of the exposures of the Fox sisters and others.

But the powers exhibited by Home when, as reported by three of the most honourable, intelligent and responsible persons in the world, he sailed through an open window out of one room seventy feet above the ground, through another open window several feet away at the same height into another room, his levitation so that he was seen apparently raised up toward the ceiling in a corner of the room, the movement of tables, playing of musical instruments without hands, rappings and automatic spellings, materializations, spirit photographs, personal identities of the dead, the sound of their voices and characteristic mannerisms of speech, mediumistic powers of such people as Mrs. Piper, Mrs. Thompson and others, these manifestations of the supernatural, the occult, are accounted for by wandering spirits who have the power to produce all such results.

They are properly called " lying " spirits.

Their delight is to lie and their business is to deceive.

A dramatic demonstration of their ability to lie and deceive is set forth in the First Book of Kings, in the twenty-second chapter.

Ahab, king of Israel, and Jehoshaphat, king of

Judah, entered into an alliance to make war against the Syrians and to recover from them the possession of Ramoth-Gilead.

Ahab gathered his four hundred prophets and inquired of them what would be the outcome of such a war.

They all with one accord bade him go up, for the Lord should deliver the battle into his hands.

Jehoshaphat was not fully satisfied. He inquired whether there was not another prophet of the Lord beside these.

Ahab answered there was such an one, Micaiah, son of Imlah, but he hated him because he always prophesied evil against him and not good. He always found him straight across his plans and purposes, seeming by his prognostications and warnings to wish to thwart him.

On the insistence of Jehoshaphat Ahab called for Micaiah.

The kings put on their robes of state, seated themselves on their thrones and waited.

The prophets came and stood expectantly before them.

One of them, Zedekiah, took horns of iron and, imitating a rush, said that in just such a manner and as easily would the king of Israel be able to go against the Syrians and push them off the land.

The prophets to a man applauded this utterance and agreed that victory would perch upon the banners of the kings.

The messenger who went to call Micaiah counselled him that he should say what all the other prophets had said, bade him speak softly and bring a smooth and easy message to the king.

But Micaiah was of altogether different stuff from that.

He was a prophet of the Lord and not man. He was called to speak the Word of God whether men should hear or forbear; whether it made them his friends or his foes.

Therefore he said:

"As the Lord liveth, what the Lord saith unto me, that I will speak."

When he came in Ahab asked him should he go up to battle at Ramoth-Gilead.

With accent of keenest irony in each word Micaiah said what the other prophets had said, bade him go up and prosper; for, evidently, the Lord intended to give him the victory, Ramoth-Gilead should certainly be his. Had not the four hundred prophets of the Lord spoken in unanimity? Could there be any doubt about it?

Ahab realized Micaiah was speaking satirically and that his message was not from the Lord. He turned upon him therefore and abjured him to speak the truth and tell the message as he had received it from the Lord and keep nothing back.

Thus abjured, Micaiah said he saw all Israel scattered on the hills as sheep that had no shepherd, and the Lord had said these had no master, let them return every man to his house, think of peace and not war. In anger and bitterness Ahab turned to Jehoshaphat and said to him:

"Did not I tell thee that he would prophesy no good concerning me, but evil?"

Then Micaiah lifted up his voice and in accents of solemn authority said:

"I saw the Lord sitting on his throne, and all the host of heaven standing by him on his right hand and on his left.

"And the Lord said, who shall persuade (deceive) Ahab that he may go up and fall at Ramoth-Gilead? And one said on this manner, and another said on that manner.

"And there came forth a spirit and stood before the Lord, and said, I will persuade him.

"And the Lord said unto him, Wherewith?

"And he said, I will go forth, and I will be a lying spirit in the mouth of all his prophets.

"And he said, Thou shalt persuade him, and prevail also: go forth and do so."

"Now therefore (saith Micaiah) behold, the Lord hath put a lying spirit in the mouth of all thy prophets, and the Lord hath spoken evil concerning thee."

Then Zedekiah, the prophet who had put on horns and showed the king how he was going to win the victory, went up to Micaiah, smote him in the face and asked him to tell which way the spirit had gone from him to Micaiah.

The king ordered Micaiah to be sent to prison and fed on bread and water till he should return victorious from the battle.

He and Jehoshaphat went up to Ramoth-Gilead and were sorely defeated. Jehoshaphat barely escaped with his life. Ahab was wounded and died.

Micaiah had told the truth.

A lying, wandering spirit had filled the mouths of all Ahab's prophets and under this lying inspiration they had given a false message to the king.

Ahab had been warned of God concerning his wickedness. He had warned him by the mouth of Elijah and told him of the evil coming upon his house.

He turned a deaf ear, was willing to listen only to that which could justify him in his unlimited wilfulness and went straight on in his iniquity as an ox to the slaughter.

When men will not take the warning and the restraint of God then the Lord gives them up to their own way.

Nothing is more pathetic and gracious than the attitude of the Lord to the waywardness of Israel; but, finally, He gives utterance to the terrible words:

" Ephraim is joined to idols: let him alone."

God uses the wickedness of the wicked as He uses the righteousness of the righteous.

He makes the wrath of man to praise Him, the remainder He restrains. He uses Satan in spite of himself as the rod of His anger and the subtilty of wandering spirits to punish those who turn their back upon His warning.

It is written:

" He that seeketh mischief, it shall come unto him."

These wandering spirits are waiting for the slightest suggestion and are ready to respond; they are on the *qui vive* to deceive.

They can personate the dead.

They can to a great degree counterfeit the identity of those who have passed into the unseen world. They cannot do it perfectly and therefore it is necessary to simulate. This accounts for the blunders and the utter silliness at times of the messages that come through the mediums, their contradictoriness and the broken links, the incoherencies; but this leads the befooled sitters in the séance to suggest unconsciously the answers they wish to receive, sometimes in the very questions they put to the mediums, more often in the surrender of the mind to the ingaze of the spirits who can thus read the very answer the listener is waiting to receive.

Let no mistake be made.

The mediums *do* speak under the influence and

powers of beings outside of themselves. It is all terribly true.

But let no further mistake be made!

It is the wandering spirit or spirits who speak through them.

Let no mistake be made, for it will, sooner or later, be costly; these wandering spirits, and these only, speak out of the unseen world and pretend to convey the message of the other side.

They are very distinct in their operation from demons.

The demons give no message, they simply come to incarnate themselves in the living; they are silent as may be possible about themselves. They seek to identify themselves with the living personality, subdue it and use it.

The wandering spirits do not enter in, possess, and make the body a habitation, they " control " the faculties of the medium as when a hypnotizer is able to make his will take the place of the will of the individual who has surrendered to him. In every case where the medium is of any avail and shows any degree of power he or she must first put himself or herself into a passive state, surrender themselves and wait for this control, make no effort in any direction to resist it. The medium as far as possible must give up every element of will or personality.

The messages from the dead are the messages of these wandering spirits more or less tinged with the mentality of the medium. This reveals the reason why some of the messages are more intellectual than others and why some are indescribable in their folly.

This must be so; otherwise as soon as an ordinarily intelligent person dies and enters the other realm he or she becomes a mental degenerate or wilfully guilty of farcical, coarse, clownish utterances that would have made them ashamed in their earthly life.

No greater demonstration of this can be had than in the book now being read by thousands everywhere, the book, " Raymond," given to the public by Sir Oliver Lodge.

Personally, the author of that book has all my most sincere and respectful sympathy.

He is a father, a bereaved father, reaching out for contact with his beloved son—a son slain while fighting on the fields of France. Every page of the book shows consciously or unconsciously his heartache, his desire to reach his boy, hear him speak in the old familiar speech and say, " Hello, Father."

I can sympathize with him.

I do not know any one who can more thoroughly, more fully and deeply sympathize.

I am a father. I have lost an only son who was an only child. My mourning for him has been what Scripture describes it to be, as " when one mourneth for an only son," putting that sorrow forward as of the most intense, the one supreme degree of sorrow.

My heart is buried in his grave. The stars have paled from the night, the sun has ceased to shine as of yore. His going has drawn a horizon over every personal plan, and though I should live a hundred years on earth it would open no vista of glories to me; and were it not that I have the sure, infallible Word of God, the light that never fails, the clear crystal message that tells me where he is, his " far better " state, the imminence of the Lord's return with him and the guaranty from God Himself that sooner or later I shall see him and we shall study the wonder of God's universe together, I would not have energy to live through the fading hours of shortest time and would without effort to retain them let the best gifts the world could offer me fall indifferently from my hand.

And because of this intensity surely no man on earth would be more predisposed than I to thrust myself outward and break, if it could be, the partition thick or thin between this world and the next and hear my son speak to me again in the voice that would be to me better than the world's best music.

And yet with all this feeling of sympathy with the father of " Raymond " I am under bonds as one put in trust with the truth of God to say that this book is the most pitiful, pathetic folly ever given to the world.

We are told of the moving of tables.

When the hands are on a table it seems like a living thing. It will move in different directions in the room. Now toward the piano, then toward the bookcase or a sewing table. When it wants a scrap book opened it will almost climb where it is and then pound so noisily and persistently that it can be quieted only by opening the book. When it is full of sympathy it will rub itself softly and gently and with an intelligent pressure against the knee of the sitter.

Raymond " came through " different mediums and with different " controls."

He speaks for himself. He speaks as Raymond. There seems to be no doubt on the part of the sitters that it is Raymond.

He gives a full description of conditions and circumstances on the " other side."

Those who " go over " are taken in hand by " spirit doctors " who build them a body suited to the new sphere.

It takes some longer than others to get a complete body.

Those who are cremated have considerable difficulty in getting entirely free from the influence or holding power of the old body. It seems more difficult to deliver the soul from the ashes of a cremated body than when it has been blown to pieces.

The doctors are very thorough so that those who have lost any member will have it restored.

Raymond has a new tooth and is rather proud of it.

He is living very comfortably.

He is living in a brick house.

The bricks are made up there, as also the things necessary to the construction of houses and streets.

The bricks and most other material used in the upper country are manufactured out of the effluvia, the gas or atoms from time to time ascending from the earth's surface.

It rains over there.

The rain is just as real as it is here.

It is just as real because it makes mud.

This mud is just as real as the rain, for it is possible to sink into it and when it touches the clothes it soils them.

They also have manure.

Why it should be there and what the source of it may be Raymond does not state; but this is evidently just as true as are all the other matters he describes.

Raymond now has a white robe such as people wear in hot countries.

When he first went over he had another suit.

This suit was manufactured out of the gas or effluvia ascending from old and rotten worsted stuff on this side.

All wool goods that get rotten here below, or just wool itself that gets old and rotten sends up a strong exhalation, and this exhalation of rotten wool produces the very best Scotch or English tweed suits as soon as it reaches the other side.

The smell of rotten and intensely putrefying things so disagreeable to us and which all sanitary organizations seek to dissipate are of enormous advantage in the upper sphere where Raymond is at present dwelling.

By these smells as they ascend from the earth the manufacturers above are able to tell what were the original forms and constructions and reproduce them; in other words, these smells are what plans and drawings of an architect are to builders.

Raymond intimates that it is necessary in the " over there " to have a good nose and a keen faculty of smell.

As soon as one goes over he finds himself more or less full of the appetites and desires he had in the earth sphere.

These appetites and desires along certain lines can be gratified on mentioning them or making application for the desired thing.

Those who are accustomed to the joy of smoking can have cigars.

There is no law of prohibition in force in that country and those who desire a brandy or whiskey soda may have one.

Flowers that fade on earth will have a resurrection. Because of the ascension of their aroma, their fragrant odours, the upper expert constructors can reproduce them.

Indeed, it would seem from Raymond's testimony there is no limit to the raw material needed, in any direction.

Domestic animals are to be found there.

Raymond says they have dogs and cats.

He is particularly interested in a " doggie " that has such a good tail. It is not a " stumpy " tail, but one having plenty of hair on it.

Sex is retained on the other side.

The man who goes over remains a man or is built up as a man.

The woman who goes over remains a woman.

They love each other with the same sincere love with which they love each other here.

Husbands and wives do not necessarily find each other or come together again.

Those who have loved each other, who have an affinity for each other will come together whether they have been husband and wife or not.   So far Raymond has seen no children born of this love.

Raymond himself does not care to eat, but some who go over have an appetite for it and there is something given to them which looks like meat.

There are laboratories in which everything used on earth can be reduplicated. This reduplication is accomplished, as already stated, by the use of the atoms of one sort or another ascending from the earth.

Raymond is particularly anxious when he tells his father about anything on the other side that he will not feel he is " sticking " him about it, but telling the absolute truth, and telling it soberly.

The climate in some respects is like our own.

There are certain parts of the day when he feels chilly, and specially since he has changed his worsted suit for the lighter garment.

Many of those who go over will not believe they are dead for a long while. It takes a long while and much patience with them before they will believe it.

Everybody, however, sooner or later, is in good form; for everybody becomes " jolly."

Raymond himself is full of his " jokes."

" Feda " the " control " represents him as rolling over convulsed with laughter.

Some of the rough characters who leave this earth sphere are taken, not to hell, for there is no hell, but to a sort of reformatory, a kind of an upper purgatory, where they are treated and come forth at last completely cured.

There are halls of learning, in which lectures in regular courses are given.

In these courses the student is taught to prepare himself for the higher spheres.

Raymond has been in one of these spheres.

There he saw a beautiful temple. It seemed to be covered with alabaster. It had stained glass windows. There were pews as in a church. It had broad aisles and people walked up and down in them seeking to put themselves in the different rays that came from the stained glass windows, the different colours signifying different states and conditions and producing them, a sort of violet ray operation.

There are towns and streets over there.

Raymond has been back to this side.   No one has ever seen him, but he has seen others.   He can see and distinguish people better at night when they are in bed; the quiet of the time and the calmness of the atmosphere facilitates the seeing of them.

The language of earth is spoken freely and the vernacular sounds familiar.   Raymond says, " by Jove," as easily as he said it no doubt when here below.

I have taken these statements from the book at random.

Their incoherencies or lack of connection are not mine.   They are as found.

Never since the art of printing was discovered and the thoughts of men placed beneath the gaze of readers was ever so pretentious a book with so compelling a theme as the state of the dead filled with such sheer nonsense, childish triviality, idiotic silliness, the brutality of excuseless vulgarity and the debauchery of clownish coarseness.

For this mass of gibbering foolery, evidential worthlessness and complete mental breakdown we are asked to give up the revelation and concept of the hereafter which the Bible brings to us.

Compare, I pray you, the Golden City, the New Jerusalem, the home of those who die in the faith of Christ, that city with its jewelled foundations, its jasper walls, its gates of pearl, its palaces and streets of gold, its river of life, its tree of life with its fruit and leaves for the healing of the nations, its shadowless light and the face of Him who created heaven and earth; who created His own new, spotless and sinless humanity; who offered it as a sacrifice for sinful men; who rose from the dead and lined the grave with the glory of His immortality; who dwells in that city as Redeemer, Saviour and spiritual life giver; compare that city and its glories with Raymond's brick house, the rain, the mud and the unspeakable manure.

Compare the Heaven of God's saints with its tall angels, with the harpers harping with their harps, with the seraphim singing their thrice holy song, "holy, holy, holy, Lord God Almighty;" that Heaven where all is righteousness, intensity of spotless purity, and where the fashion is holiness, with the heaven of spiritism, its dogs, cats, its putrefying smells, its brandy sodas, cigars and meat.

Compare the robe given to the saint who enters the upper city, the robe woven on the looms of eternal light, in the scintillating white of the essential holiness of God, with the English tweed and

worsted suits manufactured out of the effluvia, gas
or atoms ascending from the rotting and putrefying things of earth.

Compare the Bible with its rarest rhetoric, its
exalted prose, its sublime poetic expression, its
pellucid narrative, its linked logic, its supernatural
reserve, in which from one end to another you can
find neither a silly line, nor an idle phrase, the suggestion of a joke, the slightest pleasantry; this
Book that rebukes sin till its wrath flames down
like an unquenchable fire into the very intents and
purposes of the heart, withering and laying bare
every impulse that is evil; this Bible full of self-
evident and calm truthfulness, a dignity that never
breaks down, a definition and determining of right
that never compromises; this Book that is a telescope to look into eternity past and eternity to
come; a microscope that gives microscopic revelation of the smallest details of human thought and
the handiwork of God; the Book whose verifica-
tion is written in fulfilled and fulfilling prophecy,
the history of nations, the rise and fall of kings and
dynasties, cities, towns and individuals, and to so
small a detail as the fall of a wall; the Book that
is the bread of life for the dying, the water of life
for the spiritually thirsty, the wine of life, the spice
of life, milk of the simplicity of truth for the
babes in Christ and the strong meat of doctrine for
those of advanced age, of mature thought and full
experience in the exercise of the Spirit; the Book

that is simple enough for a child to read and yet
so profound, so mentally as well as spiritually
stimulating, so abysmal in its descent into essence
and causation and eternal plan and purpose that
the princes and kings in the realm of intellect and
domain of thought have been for ages digging into
its collocations, its single words, as into mines from
whose limitless deposits the wealth of fresh truth
is continually brought forth to the wonder and delight of the soul; this Book that is the alone nexus
with the personality of God, and through which
alone the Spirit can bring the consciousness of God
to the soul; this Book that has turned men from
mere animals with heads lowered to the dust, into
sweet and strengthful sons of God with uplifted
faces bathed in and made radiant with the light
reflected by it from the throne of God; compare
this Bible and its message, I bid you, with the pitiful
stuff set forth in " Raymond," and its kindred in
the literature of Spiritism as a revelation of the
unseen world, and you may well believe that it is
as far above that literature as the mountain peaks
of the Himalayas are above the grains of sand that
lie at their base, as an angel above a crawling
worm; and that this same literature of Spiritism in
its best edition and finest form is beyond all question the work of lunatics or lying, seducing, wandering spirits and the inspiration of him of whom
it is written that he is that " old serpent, called the
Devil, and Satan."

For this spiritistic literature that makes one think as he reads it of cheap vaudeville or impish pranks and hectoring tricks; for this rubbish of the dump heap of all discarded illusions of ancient days, with its naïve description of a heaven of mud, manure, putrefying smells, brandy, tobacco, dogs, cats and all the other unutterable things, we are asked to give up this Bible that alone has saved the world from despair and given hope to the sons of men.

O, it is pitiful, this story of Raymond.

It is heart-breaking.

It is heart-breaking, this book and kindred writing in the outrage of their deceptive vacuity.

To come to this book apparently authorized by a scientific mind and asking yourself, is there at last outside of the Bible a revelation that will meet the questions that rise throngingly in the soul and then find this, is as though one were smitten rudely in the face while his ears were greeted with mocking laughter.

Compare the first part of the book where a father's heart through its intense emotionalism suggests the ready answers for the watching, lurking and lying spirit waiting to personate his son through yielding mediums and their various controls; compare this part of the book where it is easily seen the father is the dupe of his own mind and the cosmic, fallen forces ready to blind him, with the last part of the book where the father himself writes of life and death, deals with them as a man of science, a man of acute intelligence, setting forth premise and drawing conclusions, and it will be seen that in this latter part you have a thinker who, whatever the faultiness of his premise, nevertheless holds himself intellectually well in hand.   Make this comparison, analyze both parts and it will be a demonstration, by the immense contrast, that in the mediumistic side of the book you have a man (giving credence to these mediumistic messages) a man who has flung aside his native, self-protecting powers of observation and reason, giving himself up blindly and without resistance to all the forces of evil which in the name of his love play upon him at their will.

The great thing upon which he and others count is that a certain photograph of Raymond of which the family is totally ignorant is revealed to them through the medium or the spirit movements of the table.   These credulous persons fail to see that all such knowledge is within the range and power of those forces the Word of God names as wandering spirits.

VII

THESE WANDERING SPIRITS ARE ALSO CALLED "SEDUCING SPIRITS"

A ND they are.

Their aim is to seduce the souls of men and lead them afar from Him who alone is the way, the truth and the life; by Whom alone any soul can find the Fatherhood of God and Sonship eternal with Him.

Nowhere is this more manifest than in the two books written by Sir Arthur Conan Doyle, the "New Revelation," and "The Vital Message." These books ought to delight the heart of every higher critic. They ought to find in them a whole arsenal of equipment for their assault upon the integrity of the Bible.

Like them, the author of the books repudiates the sacrificial value of the death of Christ.

The death of Christ as such is based upon the proposition of "original" sin and the fall of the natural man to a lower plane.

The writer of the New Revelation tells us with oracular utterance that there is no such thing as original sin. Man did not fall.

With such a conclusion unhesitatingly assumed he asks us with great simplicity, hardly worthy of the sagacity of the creator of Sherlock Holmes, if it is not plain enough to see that when sin and the fall are left out there can be no need of atonement, and since these propositions must be left out, the death of Christ has neither sacrificial nor saving value?

Christianity, he tells us, has made too much of the death of Christ. The one thing that recommends Christ to him and, as he thinks, to the world, is the life of Christ, the life as He lived it when on earth.

According to Sir Conan Doyle and the advanced men in the pulpit (who ought to crown him as head master of their kind) Christ came into the world as a great psychic, a forward sent reformer, to lay down the principles of His life that men might study and follow them. Perhaps in all the utterances and mouthings made in these days by men who would talk and teach on religious matters, there is nothing so tawdry, so shoddy like in all its accents, in all the texture of its thought as this doctrine, this slogan, this rallying cry, that we are to follow the *principles* of Christ.

The author of the books which have made him so widely known, as well as his confrères in the modern pulpit, have failed to see or are unwilling to see, that Jesus Christ did not come into this world to lay down any code of morals, any system of principles or maxims.

They fail to see, taking Him at His words as

reported in the New Testament, that He never once asked men to believe in His system, His code, or to follow and practice His principles.

He talked of salvation and damnation.

He never once said that he who should believe in and follow His principles should have eternal life and be saved.

He never once said that he who should refuse to believe in and follow His principles should die and be forever damned, miss the fellowship of God the Father and be lost forever.

He never made His principles an issue at all.

The supreme issue He set before men was— Himself.

He set Himself before men, not as truthful, but as—very Truth, essential Truth itself.

He set Himself before men as life and as the Author of life.

Since He claimed to be truth and life and the Author of life, and truth and life are found essentially only in God, He claimed to be the unique way to God, not only to God as God, but to God as the Father.

Therefore He said no man could come unto the Father but by Him.

In this statement He excluded every human being from sonship with God unless they should come by Him; and that is, by faith in Him.

He made Himself more than the way to God.

He claimed to be very God, Son of God, and as

of the essence of the Father, necessarily, God the Son.

The issue He made then was Himself, and Himself as one with the Father; so that, in asking men to believe on Him, He was asking them to believe in Him precisely as He asked them to believe in God, believe He was God, and that He was equal with Him.

Nothing could be more absolute and final than His exhortation on the night of the last supper.

Hear what He said:

" Ye believe in God, believe also in me."

He made His claim to equality with God in such fashion that there is not even the edge of a question left open in it.

He said before the world was created He sat on the throne by the Father's side, the expression of His personality and glory.

He said all the Father could do He could do.

He had life in Himself. He was self-existent.

He claimed the essential and sacred name of God.

He said, " before Abraham was—I AM."

It was because He said this the Jews took up stones to stone Him; not because He claimed pre-existence. What did that matter to them? but because He said—I AM and thus claimed that divine and sacred name as His own. He could have said, " before Abraham was I was;" but He did not; He said—I AM, and because He never made a mistake in a single utterance in His life, He said it with explicative determination.

He said He was the image of the Father—whosoever saw Him, saw the Father.

He said He was the ultimate judge of human kind.

He claimed to be the resurrection and the life. He had power to raise the dead. He could award eternal life to some men, He would ordain eternal damnation to others.

So clear and unqualified was His claim to be God that the people again took up stones to stone Him; and when He asked them why they should stone Him who had been doing such good works among them they replied, not because of any work He had done, but because, as they said:

" Thou, being a man, makest thyself God."

And they were not deceived. He did.

Whether Jesus Christ was God or only a man, only the blindest and crudest of minds could fail to see that the one thing above another He did claim was, that He was very and eternal God.

He made His personality as Son of God and God the Son the issue of eternal life and death.

He said:

" Verily, verily, I say unto you, He that believeth on me hath everlasting life."

Again He said to the people:

" If ye believe not that I am he, ye shall die in your sins."

To talk about such a man as good, if He were not actual God, is the veriest of intellectual foolery and mental self-treason of which any sane man can be excuselessly guilty.

To talk about the principles of such a man is a waste of time.

To put up such an one as an example is as gratuitous as it is wantonly childish.

Every act of good He did, He did in connection with a miracle or a claim that put Him wholly outside the range of human imitation.

To separate His miracles from His ethics; to take away His miracles and leave His character, is impossible.

If he performed them He was more than man. If He never performed them, then as credentials to His claims they fail, and His character fails with them.

But set aside His miracles—take Him as an ethical proposition alone.   What man is there who liveth who would dare to stand forth and claim as He did, that he was sinless?

Such a man would either be a self-deceived man or a deceiver; and the swiftly accumulating evidence of his human frailty, not to say sinfulness, would soon expose him.

And why talk about Him as a reformer?

What did He try to reform?

Instead of lifting His voice in condemnation of war, bidding the soldier to take off his helmet, lay down his shield and turn his sword into a plough-share, his spear into a pruning hook, He said that He, Himself, did not come into the world to bring peace, but a sword.   Even if it be argued that He meant He came to bring truth and truth would produce a division, a controversy, He knew this controversy would adjourn itself from the fire-side to the field of battle and carnage.

He never said a word against slavery.

On the contrary, He told servants to be obedient to their masters; and in those days, the average servant was a slave.

Poverty and beggary in their pitifulness met Him at every turn.   He said no word that can be taken as a protest; on the contrary, He said it would continue in the world till He should return from Heaven.   By that He meant that no institu-tion or system He should establish would cure or abolish it.

He knew labour was whiplashed by the tyranny of capital; yet, He gave no suggestion that the hours of toil should be shortened and wages in-creased.

By these statements and negative attitudes He emptied His mission of every fundamental of a reformer.

He repudiated all sound principles of exchange and money circulation when He told Peter to go catch a fish, find a piece of money in its mouth and with that pay taxes for them both.   The financier who should suggest the following of such an example would not hold his credit as a counsellor in finance long; nor would such an example if insisted on be an inspiration to toil for daily wage.

He never placed Himself forward as an advocate of thrift saving. He never told young men to lay by for the rainy day. Instead of that He told them if they would save to lay up their treasures in Heaven.

His advice concerning a highwayman or, at least, an insistent neighbour who should demand your coat that you should give him the rest of your wardrobe, would not be conducive to the cure of lawlessness nor act as an incentive to work for a living.

Judged by all the standards of reform Jesus Christ was the most impracticable man who ever lived.

He Himself never saved any money.

He did not buy a house and live in it.

He never attempted to own anything in this world.

He said the birds had nests and the foxes had holes, but He did not have a place where as owner He could even lay His head.

What then is the secret of His life?

The secret that Conan Doyle and those who think like him miss?

This is the secret.

He did not come into the world to live at all.

His miracles were not his vocation. They were simply the credentials for a local area that He was what He claimed to be and as a seal to the purpose for which He came into the world.

He came into the world but for one ultimate purpose.

Even had the Jews accepted Him as their covenant king it would have been an action that would have led to the fulfillment of this purpose.

He came into the world to fulfill a purpose, purposed from all eternity. He came into the world to die.

If the record of the New Testament is to be believed; if His own words are to be accepted— He came to die.

If He is the fulfillment of the prophecies of the Old Testament; if He responds in any wise as an antitype to all the types (and all the circumstances of His birth, His life, His deeds, His character, fit into these types and fulfill them to the letter till this certified fulfillment becomes a demonstration), then He came into the world to die as the Lamb of God, to offer Himself as a sin offering, a propitiation for the sin of the world (the sin of the first man and the nature of sin inherited by his posterity) and as an atonement for the sins and transgressions of those who by faith should so offer Him, claiming Him as a personal substitute to pay the judgment due them.

Talk too much! make too much of the death of Christ!

The whole sum and substance of Christianity lies, not in the earthly life of Christ at all, but in His sacrificial death on the cross.

What was the one theme of the Apostle Paul, the greatest preacher of Christ the world has ever had?

Was it the life the Christ of God lived when He was on earth?

Nay!

Hear what he says:

" God forbid that I should glory, save in the cross of our Lord Jesus Christ."

What was the supreme motive of his marvellous preaching?

Was it the life the blessed Son of God lived on the earth in all the perfectness of His character and the benediction of His words and deeds?

Nay!

Hear what he says for himself:

" I determined not to know anything among you, save Jesus Christ, and him crucified."

And why has our Lord Jesus Christ been exalted, made higher than the heavens and by the Father given this name of Jesus which is above every name; and why is every knee to bow to Him in heaven, in earth and under the earth; why is every tongue to confess that He is Lord to the glory of the Father?

Is it because of the beautiful and fruitful life He lived on earth?

Is it because of the splendid moral principle He laid down for mankind to follow?

Is it because He showed Himself willing to renovate society, cure its social evils and leave principles to be taught whose germinating quality should bring forth such a harvest of righteousness that the world would be gradually transformed into the kingdom of God?

Again let it be said and with all the emphasis— Nay!

Hear the reason given by the Apostle speaking under inspiration:

" Being found in fashion as a man, he humbled himself, and became obedient unto death, even the death of the cross.

" Wherefore—"

Let that " wherefore " be put in capital letters and emphasized.

" WHEREFORE:

" God also hath highly exalted him."

There you have it. Our Lord Jesus Christ has been exalted and glorified because He died on the cross.

And because He was *obedient* to the death of the cross.

To be obedient to that death He must have been commanded to die; He must have come into the world to obey that commandment and, therefore, to die and not live was the purpose for which He came into the world.

Was the commandment to die given Him of the Father?

It was.

He says so Himself.

Hear His own words:

" Therefore doth my Father love me."

Stop and let that word " therefore " arrest your attention.

Therefore is causative.

It gives us the cause of the Father's love. Why He so specially loved His Son.

Why was it? Why did He love Him?

Because of this earthly life He so perfectly lived? Because of the example He set before men? Because of the righteous and social principles He laid down for men to follow?

Let the Son of God Himself answer and put an end to all controversy:

" Therefore doth my Father love me, because I lay down my life, that I may take it again."

The Father loves Him because He lays down His life.

Why does He lay it down?

He answers that question.

" I lay down my life for the sheep." (That is, instead of the sheep.)

What shall be said of this laying down of life,

this matter of death on the cross as a commandment?

Let Him again speak for Himself:

" No man taketh it from me, but I lay it down of myself."

He was not killed—He died by His own act—by the act of His will.

" I have power to lay it down, and I have power to take it again.

" THIS COMMANDMENT HAVE I RECEIVED FROM THE FATHER."

This settles it.

He came into the world under the covenant commandment of the Father, not to live, but to die. The purpose for which He came into the world was not to live and set Himself up as an exemplar of righteousness, nor lay down principles that should revolutionize the world morally and socially. He came for none of these things.

He came to die.

He Himself said unless He should die He could be of no saving value to the world.

He said if a grain of corn did not fall into the ground and die it would bring forth no fruit.

It would abide alone.

By this He was saying simply that if He should continue to live His perfect life and then return to the Heaven from whence He came; if He left His example alone to be followed no mortal man could ever attain to it, nor would it be possible to become a partaker of that pure, spiritual and eternal life that animated Him.

He was saying that if He did not die He would be like the unplanted seed, there would be no reproduction of Himself either in life or character in the souls of men.

In saying this He was affirming what all Scripture proclaims, that man is under sentence of death, and that this sentence has been legislated against him by the righteousness of God. Not till this claim of divine righteousness was fully met could a new and spiritual life be given to the best of men.

No matter how much God might love the worst sinner and wish to save him, give him the new and worthwhile life, He could not break the demand of His own law. To do that would be to make His love the instrument of lawlessness. His love would itself become lawlessness.

Before any man could have the life in the Son of God and therefore the impetus and power of His character he must die and in dying he must fully exhaust the power or claim of death.

But it is impossible for any mere man to get beyond the extent of death.

There is no discharge in that war.

Once in the grasp of death there is no deliverance; for death is justifying righteousness as well as the life that is lived in perfect obedience to it.

As there is no limit to the demand of righteousness, there can be no limit to the extent of death that sustains it.

The only hope for any man would be that another should be willing to take his place and die in his stead.

Another!

Where could another be found?

He must be a man.

But what kind of a man?

Evidently a man against whom the law of sin and death had no claim.   Such a man of necessity must be without sin; not only in action, but in character and nature.

There is none such.   There never has been, and there never can be one of the natural race of man.

At nature evolution breaks down.   In spite of every pretension of culture human nature remains the same to-day as in the days when the Son of God walked the earth.   He said you cannot gather grapes from thorns, nor figs from thistles.   He said that which is born of the flesh is flesh and that which is born of the spirit is spirit, thereby laying down as an unchangeable law that what was born of the flesh would always be flesh, never could become spirit; and that whatever was born of spirit would always be spirit; that between them there was more than a bridgeless Atlantic Ocean difference. In no single case in the world's history has a natural man by any inhering law evolved a spiritual life. or a life that had any relation to the life of the Son of

God essentially. A Frenchman may live in all respects like an Englishman, even become a citizen of the realm of England, he never can become an actual Englishman. No matter what heights the natural man may attain morally he never can make himself a partaker of the life of the Son of God.

But even if a sinless man could be found, one against whom the law of righteousness had no claim, he never could make an atonement for man to God.

Only God can atone to God; for only that which is equal can meet that which is equal. Only God can satisfy God.

If God would atone for man then God must die. But God as God cannot die.

God could die, or taste death, only by having a nature that could die. There is only one nature God could have that would enable Him to die and meet the penalty against man, that would be a human nature.

This is the necessity and explanation of the Incarnation.

God the Son created a human nature for Himself.

It was the Son who did this because He alone of the eternal Godhead is the visibility of God; He alone has been such from all eternity—as Paul says —"in the form (therefore the appearing) of God."

He created this human nature that he might offer it both as a propitiation and an atonement.

He could make propitiation and reconcile the world to God on precisely the same principle by which the first man sinned and tore the race away from spiritual union with God.

The principle of the one for the many.

One man sinned, brought in a nature of sin and a race of sinners.

A second man who at the same time was personally God, very God, could meet the sin of the first man, reconcile the world to God and rising superior to death take the place as God the Second man, the giver of new and spiritual life to men and link them as a new race to himself as their new and eternal head.

This is why our Lord Jesus Christ came into the world to die.

This is the meaning and consequent of the death of Christ.

This was the great objective purpose of Incarnation.

When the angels sang over His birth and announced peace on earth to men of good will, they were not announcing Him as the bringer of peace to the nations as such, but as the Lamb of God who should make peace between the world and God, peace between the individual and his God; as it is written:

" Having made peace through the blood of the cross, by him to reconcile all things unto himself."

That is, by the sacrificial death of the cross, God

could reconcile the world to Himself, deal with it as under a suspended sentence and act toward it in grace; and then would the risen Christ give to every individual accepting Him as the sacrificed Lamb of God, the life and nature that should unite him in fellowship and peace with God.

Therefore it is written:

" We are reconciled to God by the death of his Son."

Talk too much about the death of Christ! Make too much of the death of Christ!

If this Bible be true, if it be not the veriest fiction that ever deceived and fooled the trusting souls of men, then every man on earth, saint or sinner, believer or infidel is living, and living only because the sacrificial death of Christ holds back judgment that grace may reign and that men taking advantage of this grace may through faith of the crucified and risen Christ receive the new life that shall link them as sons to the living God.

No greater folly was ever uttered or put into print than that too much can be made of the death of Christ.

Take it out of the Gospel and you empty the Gospel of all there is in it and make the preaching of it worse than childish folly, a deception to the souls of men and a self-arraignment and condemnation of the man who preaches it.

The failure of preachers to make much of it is

one of the signs this age of grace is drawing to its
close and that the down grade, the apostasy fore-
told, has begun.

In repudiating the sacrificial and atoning value
of the death of Christ, Sir Conan Doyle repudiates
the Christ in whom both the Old and New Testament Scriptures find their center.

The Bible knows nothing about an unsacrificial
and a mere ethically living Christ.

*He who repudiates a sacrificial Christ, repudiates
the Bible as supreme authority.*

Sir Arthur Conan Doyle has no hesitancy in doing that.

He pats it on the back and praises it that he may
feel at liberty to prove how full it is of unreliability
and contradictions.

He does this that he may deny it as final
authority.

He is under bonds to deny it as final authority
because it is continually presenting in one form or
another the necessity for the death of Christ as the
one and only way of salvation.

The Bible continually throws the fact of sin in
the face of him who reads it. Continually it announces without shedding of blood is no remission
of sin; and when it wishes to bring hope and comfort to the sinner who reads it it says: " The blood
of Jesus Christ his Son (God's Son) cleanseth us
from all sin." When it says this it is saying, as
blood violently poured out is sacrificial, it is the

sacrifice of Christ alone that can set the sinner legally clean in the sight of God.

The author of " The New Revelation " believes nothing of the kind; for he has a different view of sin from that defined in the Bible.

He looks upon sin as a matter of genital weakness.

Sin is not a criminal and vindictive attitude against God, it is purely pathological.

The slanting brow and the bulging back head must be accused and not the unfortunate personality dwelling in the unbalanced body. Genital malformation and not resident evil in the soul must bear the responsibility.

In the spiritistic system religion and faith are not factors at all.

On the other side of the grave all faiths, all religions, no religion and no faith, Idolater and Christian, Romanist and Protestant all arrive at the same place and in the same general good condition.

The question of sin is not raised.

Since according to Sir Conan sin is wholly a matter of material construction the moment the soul is relieved from the body all those attitudes and actions are negatived, the freed soul has no consciousness of them.

It is because of this utter evacuation of the idea of sin in relation to the soul or the individual that no issue of faith or religion, and in reality, if the matter be pressed to its conclusion, no issue of

right or wrong as set up by religious standards can
have any place on the other side.

In the nature of the case religious faith and de-
votion can have no special reward and unbelief
can have no punishment.

There is no punishment on the other side.

There is no such thing as hell.

As one of the spiritistic leaders says:

" The joy of heaven is the emptying of hell."

Sir Conan Doyle cannot believe in hell because
the Bible proclaims it, but he can believe in a pell-
mell heaven in behalf of those who are *fitted for
hell* because a tilting table tells him in spasmodic
knockings there is one.

In giving us " The New Revelation " and in
turning away from the Bible, the author is willing
to accept the most unsubstantial evidence concerning the unseen world and the state of the dead.

Never have I anywhere in all the wide range of
my reading and observation seen such childlike
faith and willingness to accept any miracle proclaimed or perpetrated in séances—a faith that in
reality borders on the surrender of the most ele-
mentary conditions of reasoning and logic.

Here then are two men!

Both representatively intelligent.

The one, a scientist with developed tendencies to
metaphysics, the other, a man of high creative
imagination and constructive literary genius; both
of them in the grip of a thing which reveals in

them side by side with their sound reasoning a
credulity and blindness intensely pathetic and
terrible. Pathetic, because of the helpless, unre-
strained way in which they allow themselves to be
submerged by spiritistic delusion. Terrible, because of the soul-destroying consequences not only
to themselves, but by their example, to others.

To all statements they may make, to all reasons
they offer as cogent, to every fact they present,
there is one all sufficient answer—and that is:

Wandering spirits.

Lying and seducing spirits.

It is the fulfillment of the prophecy made of long
date and already quoted:

" Now the Spirit speaketh expressly that in the
latter times, certain ones shall apostatize from the
faith, giving heed to wandering spirits, and to the
teachings of demons, speaking lies in hypocrisy."

VIII

THE SUFFERING OF THE CHRISTLESS DEAD IS DUE TO THEIR DISCARNATE STATE

THE proof of this is to be found in the story of the demoniac of Gadara.

The spokesman of the spirits in the man cried out:

" What have I to do with thee, Jesus, thou Son of God most high. I beseech thee, torment me not."

This is a startling cry.

Listen to it again:

" I beseech thee, torment me not."

Why did he cry that?

What torment did he expect from the Son of God?

The explanation is given in the following verse.

We are told he made this beseeching plea because the Lord had commanded the spirit and his companions to come out of the man.

To be out of the body, then, to be discarnate was the torment against which the demon protested.

This is in the nature and logic of the constitution of man.

Man is a threefold being. He is spirit, soul and body.

The soul is the person.

Spirit and body are the agents.

When a person dies spirit and soul are not separated.

They go out of the body together.

The spirit becomes henceforth the vehicle of the soul, the instrument of its expression. This is the reason why the disembodied soul is so frequently spoken of as a spirit.

All the appetites, desires, sensations, every emotion are centered in the Soul.

It is not the body or any of its nerves that are subject to sensation at all. These are means to convey sensation to the soul. The soul alone feels. A dead body has no feeling of any sort. A few moments before death the individual is conscious of pain and may locate it in some part of the body, but the sensation is in the soul. A second after death there is no response in the body, it does not resent or resist that which would have made it quiver before. Wherein is the difference? Shall it be said it is the absence of breath from the lungs? But you can go into a chemical laboratory and manufacture the very breath that aforetime was in the lungs. You will have breath, but you will not have life, you will not have personality. Even if you could open the eyes and force the vocal organs mechanically to speak there would be no individualism there; nor would there be any indication of feeling. That body with all the reanimation you could give it would have no sensation. There is only one decent conclusion, something more than breath was in that body before. That something was a some one, a person, and it was the some one, the person we call a soul, that in that body previously was happy or sorrowful, felt pain and suffered.

Make no mistake about it—all feeling and therefore all appetites, all emotions and desires of every and any kind are exclusively in the soul, the person.

As these emotional conditions do not remain in the body when the soul goes out of the body then the soul takes its emotions, its appetites, its desires and its capacity of sensation with it.

The appetites and the desires are all there, just the same and just as intense and in one sense more than when in the body. This is so because the mechanical construction of the body sometimes gives out as when a telephone wire or an electrical transmitter is out of order. If an arm or a foot is paralyzed while the individual is alive he does not feel sensation through either of those members. At death the soul is freed from whatever atrophy of sensational transmission may have been in the body. The moment freed the resident sensation, whatever it is, manifests itself.

All this is true because the soul is not a mere nimbus. It has form, and the form is the same as the body. Daniel speaks of his body as a sheath, a scabbard.   Just as the scabbard is in a degree the form of the sword within it, so is the body in a degree the indication of the soul in it.   The soul in the new state of disembodiment is, paradoxical as it may seem, but nevertheless true, more keenly sensitive than ever.

The man who drank whiskey wants whiskey.

The man and woman who have given themselves up to lust while here, find themselves burning and mad with their lusts when out of the body.

This accounts for and explains the demand of the rich man that Lazarus should come and dip his finger in water and cool his tongue.

It is not a question whether there was any water or whether there was any tongue.

The fact is the man had in his soul the sensation of thirst and in calling out for its gratification he used the terms of his earth existence.

The spirit has no functional powers with which to meet the sensation of the soul with respect to its earth sphere desires.

The body is gone.

Here is the agony, the torment, to say nothing of the mental and moral side of it.

Appetites, desires growing more and more intense because not satisfied.

And no way to satisfy them.

Disembodied—discarnate—that is, indeed, frightful.

And here is the meaning and logic of death at last.

Embodiment is natural.

It is the completion of man.

It was given him in original creation because God intended him to live, not in Heaven or some other sphere, but on earth.

Had not man sinned and fallen his body would have been made immortal.

His multiplication would have eventually reached its limit and the population of earth remained stationary and eternal. Only after the fall was the conception of the woman multiplied, only after death came in and made it necessary that each generation should be replenished.

Death is not natural.

It is a violation of nature.

It could not come except by the will of God. Since He wills it and it is unnatural, a violation of the law of embodiment, then it is an imposition from God, and as such is a sentence and a punishment.

As death removes the individual from the earth sphere it ought to be seen without much difficulty that it is not an issue of the continuance of the soul but a change in the sphere of existence of the soul, and along with it the mode of existence.

Death therefore is the banishment of man from the sphere of the earth.

The banishment of man from the habitat originally given him of God.

He is removed from the earth sphere by the death of his body.

Death therefore has no relation to the existence of the soul.

Death has to do with the mechanical construction called the body; that body which in Scripture is called a house of clay, a tabernacle, a temple, a tent, an earthen vessel, a garment, a robe; that body which at death Scripture says is taken down as one takes down a tent; that body out of which at death the soul of the believer in Christ goes with the assurance of Scripture that it will have another building, a house not made with hands; that body out of which the believer in Christ is said to go as from the home of the soul on earth to the home with the Lord in Heaven.

The soul of the person who is not united to Christ at death is removed into a condition that is not only abnormal, but painful.

He enters into a state for which he was never intended in so far as construction is related to the soul.

There is nothing to respond to his constitution.

It is a condition aggravated by the degree of moral or immoral life the individual has lived while on earth.

But even though the individual should be the most moral man who ever lived, out of Christ, he must suffer his abnormal condition of disembodiment.

If it be asked why does not a Christian suffer from the same abnormal condition of disembodiment, the answer is: if the professed Christian be a genuine believer he is united to the risen and glorified body of the Lord; as it is written:

" We are members of his body, of his flesh, and of his bones."

And again:

" He that is joined to the Lord is one spirit."

When the Christian dies he finds his articulation with the body of Christ realized; as out of that body he has received his spiritual life and nourishment while on earth; so the moment of disembodiment he finds the body of his Lord a resource in sustaining his new condition.

He finds his oneness with the Spirit of Christ the delivering power from the insatiable desires of the old nature.

There is nothing but the purifying consciousness of his oneness with Christ.   This oneness now fills him with the desires that the glorified Christ can transmit to him without hindrance.

Nor is this all—

According to the sixth chapter of the Revelation, so soon as the liberated soul is in Heaven it receives and is clothed upon with a white robe.

The fact of this robe is a twofold demonstration. It proves the soul has form—a robe cannot be put on that which has no form; to talk about it would be senseless and trifling.

It proves the robe is material of a kind, for that which is wholly immaterial is not placed upon that which has form, nor is it visible. The white robe is a temporary materialization, but not of flesh. It is not the resurrection body, but a manifestation and visualization till the resurrection hour and the restitution of the body for the earth sphere again.

IX

THE FUTURE SUFFERING OF THE CHRISTLESS DEAD WILL BE ENDLESS DISEMBODIMENT

THIS is forecast in the question of one of the demoniacs of Gadara.

There were two.

The spirit in one of them besought the Lord in the name of his companions not to cast them out and torment them by this fresh act of disembodiment.

The other asked the Lord an immense and far-reaching question.

He said:

" What have we to do with thee, Jesus, thou Son of God? Art thou come hither to torment us before the time?"

As torment to them meant disembodiment, and they had previously been disembodied by death; as this embodiment in living other persons was temporary, it could refer only to another period of disembodiment and therefore to a period of embodiment of their own before that.

Such a condition would call for the resurrection of these spirits, a restoration of body and then death again in their own proper bodies.

Is there such a thing taught in Scripture?

There is.

Our Lord Jesus Christ has said that all that are in their graves shall come forth. The word for graves signifies the burial places of the bodies. He is speaking of resurrection of the body. He says there will be two resurrections, the resurrection of those who are His and the resurrection unto damnation; that is the resurrection unto final judgment.

This resurrection unto damnation or judgment is called " the rest of the dead." It takes place at the great white throne. It occurs a thousand years after the resurrection of the saved.

It is the Second Resurrection.

The dead out of Christ will be brought forth from hades.

Bodies will again be given to them.

They will be assembled before this great white throne and judged for the deeds done in the body.

The sentence which previously condemned them to disembodiment will be confirmed.

They will be sent forth to die the second time.

This time they will die by fire.

Their bodies will be consumed.

Our Lord has said the soul cannot be killed. To kill is to take away life, existence. He says the soul cannot be killed, therefore existence cannot be taken from it. The word " kill " is never applied to the soul. The word " destroy " is; but while the word "kill" has but one meaning, "destroy" has more than one meaning, it may mean moral and spiritual destruction and is so used in Scripture; since the word "kill" cannot be used in relation to the soul and the word "destroy" is so used, and our Lord says the soul cannot be killed, existence cannot be taken away from it, then destroy when applied to the soul cannot mean the non-existence of the soul.

As the body will be destroyed and the soul will never cease to exist; as after the death of the body there will be no resurrection, then the soul will remain in a state of disembodiment forever.

The soul will be an eternal ghost.

It will no longer be able to incarnate itself. Forever it must remain invisible. Forever it must continue as a derelict of humanity.

It may be asked, if the body is to be destroyed, where is the fire of which the Son of God so terribly speaks, calling it "hell-fire," where the fire is not quenched and the worm dies not?

The answer is, there is a literal fire and a spiritual fire.

The Apostle James speaks of the spiritual fire.

He says the tongue is set on fire of hell.

The word "hell" is "gehenna," and gehenna means the lake of fire, the second death.

Literally therefore James says:

The tongue is set on fire of the lake of fire.

You know and every one knows that literal fire

never has and does not now burst out in flame in or on a man's tongue.

It is not a figure of speech, it is a fact; but, it is a spiritual fire.

This spiritual fire is sin; as it is written:

"Men—*burned* in their lust one toward another."

This is a fire that will burn forever in the unregenerate soul, the fire of sin.

Nor is this an interpretation of imagination, it is the authoritative announcement of the Son of God.

Speaking of those who should sin against the Holy Ghost that they never should have forgiveness of sins, He warns of the danger of " eternal damnation."

Literally, " subject to eternal sin."

That means forever under the power of sin; forever under bonds to sin.

But again it may be asked how is it possible for a soul to sin without a body.

The answer is—sin is not in the body at all.

" Every sin that a man doeth is without the body."

The word " without " means " outside."

Sin is outside the body, it is apart from, and finds its source and area independently of, the body.

Sin is in the arena of the mind and under the operation of the will.

Sin, therefore, is not an expression of organs,

but personality; and since the soul is the person—
sin is in the soul.

This is a complete refutation of the doctrine set
forth by Sir Conan Doyle, that sin is a matter of
physical construction.

No! sin is in the soul.   It is not the body, but the
soul, the person, who sins, and whatever sin is committed by the body is committed by it as the agent
of the soul.   The soul when it sins deteriorates the
body.   It is not the body that wears out the soul,
but the soul that wears out the body.   As a consequence of its powers of impression on plastic
matter the soul can so impregnate the body with
its sin state that the body will become almost quick
enough in its organism to suggest, or, at least, to
meet instantly the thought of sin suggested by the
soul.

The disembodied soul then in eternity will go on
sinning, not in the exercise of it through bodily
functioning, but by increased culture of desire in
the mind.

Eternal sinning in the mind, the development of
desire with no means of gratification, means nothing less than eternal suffering.

This is the eternal and unquenchable fire against
which the Son of God so intensely warns.

What then is the worm that dieth not?

Listen to that word of Abraham to the lost rich
man in hades:

"Remember!"

Memory is a blessed gift. It can bring back the days of old, the scenes of joy, the face we loved, the smile that greeted us, the happy and caressing voice; and it shall be as though they died not, were alive and we felt again the kiss upon the lips, the pressure of the missing hand and walked with them as in the olden time before death's sunless shadow fell upon our way or the icy breath of the tomb had withered, almost, every flower of hope within us.

But memory is a torture—a torture when it brings back days of joy that can come no more, the vision of hope forever fled, the brooding wings of black despair, lost opportunities, the fatal step that missed the road, the red sin, the "damned spot" that will not out, the regret, the remorse that bites and gnaws, and ever bites.

Is there a more deathless worm than that—a memory like that?

And to the helplessly and hopelessly lost soul Abraham said:

"Remember!"

The sudden death of the body and its complete destruction in the literal lake of fire is terrible enough in the fact that it is the end of all hope the individual will ever again have a body.

It would be terrible enough to be condemned to be a ghost, a mere shadow flung against the wall of eternity with no powers of manifestation; but to have all the function of the soul as when on earth,

to think, desire, to be filled with all the strivings
and intents of a personality that the longer it exists
the more intense it becomes as a personality, if by
nothing less than the effort at expression and culture which it must make, this is unspeakable and is
not merely the direct action of God in imposing the
penalty, but the price and peril that is involved in
the very creation of a personality outside of God
Himself.   The eternal God was forced in the nature of things to make a personality with all the
risks that must go with it of free exercise of will to
a certain point, or else make a machine; and this
would have been no better in the long run, nor so
good as to have made a tree.   In His determination to create " fellows " who should be the recipro-
cation of His own personality like so many living
mirrors that would reflect Him and glorify Him in
His own character and, at the same time (to use
the phraseology of earth), find the companionship
that would deliver Him from the isolation of Himself in Himself, He must take the infinite risk of
those personalities becoming their own eternal ruin.
The grace of the redemption that is in Christ Jesus
is the rift in the cloud and otherwise darkness, and
carries with it to the Church of Christ, if it can
see, the emphasis of the immense responsibility that
God in His necessity (to speak as a man) has laid
upon it.

Great is the warning the Son of God gives.

The terms are in the emphasis of material things.

Better He says it will be to take part in the first resurrection with one eye, or one foot (and therefore He says pluck out the eye and cut off the foot if it shall endanger your part in that resurrection) than to have a perfect body and take part in the second resurrection unto the second death, eternal disembodiment and the fire of ungratified sin forever in the soul.

And this fact of eternal sinning proclaimed and avouched by Him who is the eternal headquarters of eternal truth sets aside and settles forever all fallacious suggestions of a " second chance."

As death finds us eternity keeps us.

The major fact of eternal discarnation and along with it the eternal sinning explains the strange and terrible cry of the second one of the demoniacs:

"Art thou come hither to torment us before the time?"

They knew of the second resurrection and the second death and all that it meant. They knew that then all hope of materialization would be over throughout endless eternities.

They and all the rest who go over into that prison house of the lost know it to-day.

There are no illusions in that hell which is hades; that hades which is the vestibule of gehenna.

X

THE CHRISTIAN ALONE WILL HAVE ETERNAL EMBODIMENT

THIS embodiment will take place at the Second Coming of our Lord Jesus Christ. He will descend into the upper air.

With the shout of omnipotence He will, and with the same ease with which He created the first body from the dust, cause the seed planted in the body of the Christian dead (and held by the Holy Spirit in union with the glorified body of the Lord) to burst forth and bloom in the identity of the old, and the beauty of a new, and glorious, body.

To this body He will unite the soul of the Christian He brings with Him.

Then will that Christian for the first time become *immortal*.

Here then is the meaning of immortality—not continued existence, that is assured for all souls good or bad, but a deathless, incorruptible body in the image and likeness of the Son of God Himself.

Since the Coming of the Lord for His saints precedes His appearing in glory with them; and as that special and precedent Coming is not like the appearing in glory, dependent on the fulfillment of certain predicted events, but may be at any moment, then as Christians we are always standing on the threshold of immortality; for, when He comes to raise those who have fallen asleep in His name the living who believe in Him will not die, but be changed immediately, in the twinkling of an eye, into the same image.

This is the meaning of that great saying of the Lord to the sister of Lazarus:

" I am the resurrection and the life; he that believeth in me, though he were dead, yet (when I come) shall he live:

"And whosoever liveth and believeth in me (when I come) shall never die."

In all this our Lord in the nature of the case is speaking of the body.

This is evident by the last statement:

" Whosoever liveth and believeth in me shall never die."

Christians who live and believe do die as the resurrection proves.

The Lord is therefore speaking of the time when His Coming will make it impossible to die by reason of the transfiguration of the body of the believer into His likeness.

This is the declaration of the Apostle Paul.

He writes:

" Behold, I shew you a mystery; (that is, he now reveals the mystery—makes known that which has been a great secret) we shall not all sleep (not all die) but we shall all be changed.

" In a moment, in the twinkling of an eye, at the last trump: for the trumpet shall sound, and the dead shall be raised incorruptible, and we shall be changed."

And this is at the Coming of Christ for His saints; as it is written:

" They that are Christ's at his coming."

From all this it follows sons of God and sons of God alone will have immortality.

That is to say, sons of God and sons of God alone of the human race will be forever incarnate, forever shining in the image and likeness of the Lord, filled with His glory and endowed with His powers.

Wherefore the Apostle writing to the Philippians says:

" For our conversation (citizenship) is in heaven; from whence also we look for the Saviour, the Lord Jesus Christ:

" Who shall change our vile body (the body of our humiliation—limitation) that it may be fashioned like unto his glorious body (body of glory) according to the working (energy, power) whereby he is able to subdue all things unto himself."

Nor is this to be all; after the kingdom is established and He has had his final dealings with the dead that do not know His name the Lord will cause this old earth to pass through purifying fires, renovate it, swing it under a new heavens, make it a new earth and then come back with all the redeemed to fulfill the true purpose for which the earth was created, to make it the eternal home and dwelling place of a race of immortal, glorified men, each man an enthronement of God and a revelation of the grace of our Lord Jesus Christ, His image and glory.

This is a concept worthy of God and worthy of man.

It stands over in splendour against the pitifulness of the spiritistic concept, its beggary on the one side, its utter vacuity, and its deception on the other; over against the incoherencies of its counter-feiting forces and the subtlety with which it shuts out from the soul the peril that awaits all who are not in union with the risen Christ.

XI

WE HAVE A FULL REVELATION CONCERNING THE CHRISTIAN DEAD

WE know where they are.

The moment they are out of the body they are in the third heaven, in the country called Paradise, in the place the Son of God went to prepare, the city which Paul says was prepared in his day, the Holy City which John under divine inspiration so wonderfully describes.

The moment they enter they are clothed with the white robe that makes them visible to one another.

They are with the Lord.

Three simple words—With the Lord.

But what a world of meaning in those three.

Consider the Lord if you will in His earthly, human life as He lived it here—full of the beauty of unselfishness, the grace of tender compassion, speaking words that fell into the hurt of the soul as balm that never was in Gilead. Consider Him, bidding the weary and the heavy laden to come to Him in the assurance that He would give them rest, not merely rest of body, but rest of soul. Consider Him as He says, "him that cometh unto me I will in no wise cast out." Consider Him as with unlimited power He heals the sick, raises the dead, stills the storm!

To be with Him! what privilege could be more blessed than that?

What greater resource of knowledge, consolation and certitude of life worth while could there be than to be with Him?

The Apostle writing by the inspiration of God says the believer who dies is " absent from home out of this body and immediately at home with the Lord."

" Home! "

What a word that is!

Not in some stranger country, exposed to the cold tolerance of others, shut up to narrowness, to sore limitation; but at home walled in from every assaulting force, from every wagging, careless tongue and misconception, from the disintegrating influence of sordid things that would buy and sell you, cheapen you and leave you worthless in the end.   At home in close and intimate relation with Him who died for us, in the joy and fellowship of His presence who for us men and our redemption for a while walked a homeless stranger here.

And because of all He is to those who go hence in His name the Apostle says:

" I have a desire to depart and be with Christ— which is—far better."

" Better " is a comparative.   A comparative is the extension of the positive of the quality of good.

It means that death to the Christian is not a disaster.

No! Hear what the Apostle says:

" For me to live is Christ, and to die is gain."

It means that life takes on a progression in essence, in character and knowledge.

It is a sphere above that of earth life as earth life is now.

It is described in Holy Scripture as a state of " rest."

Rest does not mean sleep or unconsciousness.

It is harmony, refreshment, the soul finding its true center of moral, spiritual and intellectual gravity around the glorified person of the risen Lord.

They live in the company of the best, the bravest and the true of earth, the aristocrats of eternity; those who have been twice born, who trace their ancestry back to the covenant grace and eternal purpose of God; those who lived the life that counted for God, and because it counted for God counted for man; those who hated sin and loved righteousness, out of their own sorrows poured the cup of healing into the wounds and sorrows of others, glorified the mercy that forgave their own failures and lifted them steadily day by day out of self into Christ, into the consciousness of God in whom they joyed with joy exceeding and full of glory.

Those who depart now into the company of the blest, the purified, those who are rising upward ever more into the felicity of life that finds its compensation in the activities of mental, moral and intellectual growth.

They hear the speech that Paul heard when he was caught up into the third heaven and into paradise, words which his mortal tongue could not repeat without stumbling.

They speak that speech which utters the soul at its best. Down here there are moments when the vocabulary of earth has to give way to the unwritten, unspoken speech of the soul finding its true accents alone in Heaven.

According to the sixth chapter of the Revelation which gives an account of the martyred dead they are interested in those from whom they have parted here below on these tear-stained shores of time.

The angels of God who in the book of the Revelation are represented as the messengers of the redeemed bear back report of the things of earth. If that report should bring sadness, the Lord, we are told, will wipe away all tears from their eyes and give them an assuagement of grief He alone can give. He who once wept on earth will know how from His own tears to distill the comfort that shall antidote the keenest sorrow.

Whatever genius those who depart had here on earth they will have there, but multiplied in its power.

All endowment of God finds its enlargement when they pass from hence. Here men have mental endowments, but not always the powers of expression. I once knew a man with great powers of thinking and reason. He had great visions of things; but his vocabulary was painfully limited. His ideas came searching for words as when a blind man gropes for the wall. The ideas were there and they were far in advance of the average man of his surroundings, but they were strangled and fell short of the expression they required. The soul of that man freed from its " muddy vesture " could, at least, impress itself on the mind of a kindred soul in the upper country; just as here and there in this life people intuitively understand each other with, perhaps, a word or a look or a pressure of the hand.

" Better " applies in every degree of endowment.

The Scientist is a better scientist.

The Artist a better artist.

The Musician a better musician.

The Mathematician finds himself in his element confronting the fact that the whole universe is a mathematical problem; that all things go back to numbers, degrees and measurements.

Life there is not a droning nor a dream, but rich activity of the unfolding soul.

The truths of redemption are seen in the clarity of the Lord's presence. They look forward to the hour when the Lord shall bring them back and give them the bodies that belong to them; they know these bodies were bought by blood and sealed by the Holy Spirit; for His sake who purchased them at such a price as well as their own they want Him to come and show Himself victor over the grave.

And here, indeed, is the great objective of redemption, to make man as God intended him, a three-fold being, the continual proclamation of the divine Triunity.   The Lord God might give them bodies of a new and distinct creation, but it would rob Him of His own openly proclaimed glory as the resurrection as well as life.   To leave Christians in Heaven or even to bring them forth in their white-robed glory would at the best be but a makeshift, with it all they would be only materialized ghosts. Eternal disembodiment is the state of the unredeemed.   For a single body that had once been the temple of the Holy Ghost to remain as a temple overthrown and fallen in the dust would be a scandal to the Son of God in that He Himself rose from the dead and gave solemn promise of resurrection to all who should fall asleep in His name and failed to raise them, failed to make all, whether dead or living, like Himself—immortal.

Those in Heaven, whatever their failure to apprehend it while on earth, now know that this resurrection of the " dead in Christ," and transfiguration of the living in Him is His special glory. They know that this will be His joy and that He is coming forth to accomplish it; to them this Coming is now as they never dreamed or realized it to be—" That Blessed Hope."

They look forward to the hour when earth shall again be their home, a perfect earth freed from the stain of sin and tears, of the shadow of death and the darkness of the grave; when it shall be a text-book as well as a home out of which they shall ceaselessly learn of the genius and the glory of Him who in the beginning framed it and made it to be inhabited forever; a world of transcendent beauty and an immortal race of God-men whose every joy of achievement should be a fresh proclamation to the glory and grace of Him who redeemed them.

Here is a revelation concerning the Christian dead that is full and satisfying.

What folly to turn away from it, so songful and assuring to aching hearts, so self-evidently true and commending itself to the mind and intellect, so lifted above the inane and trivial, so rich with the wealth of a divine concept, to such a book as " Raymond," with its incoherent babbling, its worse than foolishness, its heart-breaking emptiness and repellent commonness; what folly to turn away from the revelation of God to that; or, to the " New Revelation," " The Vital Message," to find in them again the guess, the imagination and unbelief of man, repudiation of the cross of Christ, the blood of redemption and the Holy Word of God.

XII

WE HAVE, ALAS, A FULL AND COMPLETE REVELATION CONCERNING THE CHRISTLESS DEAD

WE know too well where they are, what they are and what the future holds in store for them.

We know enough to make us shudder and shrink back; we know enough to bid us go forth and sound the alarm in no uncertain terms and with tenderness and tears and all praying warn those who stand upon the edge of their days with only a heart-beat between them and an irrevocable eternity—an eternity without Christ.

Can you conceive of anything more terrible than for a human being in the midst of life with utter indifference to the future, too absorbed in the fleeting present of time to think of eternity, suddenly wrenched out of life and taken without one touch of Christ in the soul into the limitless beyond?

In bidding good-bye to the Ephesian pastors the Apostle told them he had not shunned to declare unto them and the people of Ephesus the whole counsel of God; he felt his skirts clear from the blood of all men because for three years and a half he had preached and warned them night and day with tears. Paul was not a man given to mere emotionalism. You will look in vain for any exaggeration in his life; it was high and sustained at a pitch of unfailing intensity, but in all soberness and truth.

So terrific was the thought of the doom awaiting those out of Christ, so heavily did the soul interest of his kinsmen according to the flesh press upon his heart that he declared himself willing to be accursed from Christ if thereby he might be able to save some.

Nothing in speech is more terrible than the words of the softest spoken man who ever lived, the tender compassionate Son of God. He it is who coined the word " hell-fire " and warns men that it would be better to mutilate the body and enter with it into the kingdom of God than, as has already been said, with a perfect body to go into that second death from which the soul will emerge forever a wandering, hapless and hopeless ghost.

But with all words that can be gathered and every accent of terror that may be put into them nothing looms up on the horizon of time with such meaning and warning as the cross of Christ itself. Nothing echoes with such immensity and intensity as the cry of the forsaken one, the far reach of His question, " My God, my God, why hast thou forsaken me ? "

He was forsaken and was left dying there as an absolutely self-deceived victim of His own imagination; or, He was there in fulfillment of the eternal purpose of God, and as the divinely appointed substitute for man in the down sweep of the wrath of God that poured over Him as the representative of man under judgment echoed the agony and surprise that will come from the soul of every human being, finally, who has not accepted the grace which that cross reveals.

There is no need for any further revelation concerning the dead out of Christ. We know enough to make us as professed Christians up and doing with the means at our command to save men, not merely for the poor thing that is filling the air, called " social service," but save men for Christ here and for their own eternal welfare when time shall have passed beyond the count of years. We know enough to make us do that or to put our Christianity where it belongs, a mere profession without meaning to God or man.

XIII

LET ME WARN YOU NOT TO SEEK TO THE DEAD FOR INFORMATION

LET me in no uncertain terms warn every soul to flee from Spiritism. Under no circumstance to seek to tamper with the unseen world or endeavour to have communication from the dead.

Let me warn every unsaved person that in doing so you yield yourself to the influence and power of lying spirits who will hide from you the awful fate of discarnation to every one out of Christ. They will hide from you the terrific fact that once disembodied, hope is gone; that only the second resurrection, second death, eternal sinning, eternal desires forever unquenched, are in store for you.

Above all, let every Christian shun this Satanic and perilous ground. No more think of having an ouija board in your home or fooling with it, or being tempted to put your hands on tables in nervous anticipation with others of more or less psychic force than you would invite the arch-enemy of God and man to dwell intimately with you.

There is no need that any human being should seek to inquire of the dead.

There is no need to do so because we have a full and complete revelation from God concerning the state of the dead.

The moment you tamper with the unseen world in never so small a way you put yourself on Satan's ground.

You throw yourself open to the invasion of lost souls, the demons, who now and then break jail and come forth to find the human bodies that may give relief to their intolerable woe.

You throw yourself open to the power and duplicity of wandering spirits who will fool and deceive you, hold you in a clutch of fascination from which all the wisdom and sometimes the power of God fails to deliver the souls that surrender to them.

A woman of high standing and intellectual culture recently gave herself up to the temptation of the ouija board. The inoffensive thing held her night and day. Again and again she would retire and determine to forget it in sleep. She could not sleep. She would call for the board and give herself up to it through the hours of the night till the wan light of the morning.

She could not escape its claims.

To-day she is in a home for the insane and her calls for that plaything that has chased reason from its throne are heartrending.

Insanity lies over on the ground of Spiritism, lurking there in the power of the wandering spirit to seize upon the best mind and make it a pitiable wreck.

Once when a boy I saw a young woman, a raving maniac. Her hair that had been slightly auburn seemed to flow back from her forehead like a stream of living fire. Her face was so strangely white it sickened me to look at it. Her eyes blazed with an infernal light. Her mouth was thick with bloody foam. She gnashed her teeth like a wild beast till it sounded as the grinding and crunching of human bones. She tore her clothes in an unspeakable recklessness from her rare, beautiful body. She cursed as no man could curse till the blood in me seemed to freeze. She tried to kill others and then tried to kill herself. Strong men fought with her in the endeavour to place her in the car that should take her to the asylum. She was but a frail, delicate girl and yet she flung those men, a half dozen of them, almost as if they had been wisps of straw; and not till, suddenly, some one slipped the straight jacket over her head pinioning her arms helplessly to her side, could they at all control her and then at the last they bound her about the body with strong cords.

Something more than mere insanity was hers.

If ever a human being was possessed with a demon she was.

To yield yourself to Spiritism is to throw the door open through which many have passed into the atmosphere and realm of immorality.

A certain young woman of the most exceptional purity in thought and character was led to experiment with an ouija board.

She was amazed to find she had what is called " the psychic force."

Messages began to come thick and fast.

At first they were perfectly harmless. They were mysterious. They revealed some things known only to herself. Many of the things that came through she was able to verify. The idea that she stood, so to speak, on the very edge of another world and could hold communication filled her with amazement and delight. She looked at the sun of day and the stars of night with new concept. Back of all these seen things was that hitherto unknown world. What a vista was open to her mind. The thought that she might come in contact with some of the great ones in the beyond completely fascinated her.

Then little by little the messages began to change their character. Suggestions came that in a measure surprised her; but they were vailed. Nevertheless they left a tumult in her mind and her pulses beat with a new force, she felt the blood in her veins oftentimes grow hot as with a sudden, strange heat.

The messages grew bolder, from suggestions they grew to open statements, they became daringly tempting and openly obscene.

In horror she flung the board from her and hid

her face in her hands while her heart seemed to bound out of her and her breath came quick and short.

For several days she would not look at the thing, the memories of it haunted her; but it had a fascination she could not escape. She went back to it. She listened to it. It continued its terrible messages.

She found herself listening to them, learning things she never dreamed, filled with curiosity and desire that shamed and horrified her and yet held her, till in a sudden moment of temporary lull in the message, she sprang to her feet, cast the board on the floor, stamped on it and crushed it, crying, "I am lost, I am lost." She was delivered, but the memory of it was as though she had passed through a sewerage of human corruption.

She is not the only one into whose mind the poison of wandering spirits has been poured.

B. F. Hatch, at one time a spiritualist, author of "Spiritualism Exposed," declares he knew in his day of seventy mediums leading irregular lives, some in open license, and gives description thereof in terms not necessary to repeat.

Nor is this altogether surprising.

When once the mind is thrown open to the powers on the borderland of this world and the unseen, the individual is liable to the double assault of demons from the pit and wandering spirits from the dark zone.

The very principle which underlies Spiritism that there is no sin essentially considered; that responsibility for any irregularity in life does not lie with personality, but with the physical construction, and what is called sin is simply the response to the needs of that construction, is bound sooner or later, in one direction or another, to undermine the most rigid concept of personal righteousness.

When it is believed, as Sir Arthur Conan Doyle's book would seem to teach, that the believer and the unbeliever, servant of God and servant of unrighteousness, infidel and Christian, all go to the same place, that there is no final accounting for the life lived here; that even though the soul that crosses over may not reach the highest plane at once, it will, nevertheless, at last, pass on and up into the most satisfying and delightful of experiences—all this underlying idea is bound, inevitably, to break apart the armour of righteousness and render vulnerable the soul most exacting in rightness.

It is the little crevice by and by widening into the larger fissure that opens the building to its final fall.

Spiritism leads to the denial of " the faith once for all delivered to the saints."

The Word of God speaks of the wandering spirits as " seducing " spirits.

As the Apostle writes, and as we have seen, they lead to apostasy.

Those who yield to the call from the unseen;

who accept manifestations through mediums; who really believe what they profess; who are sure the dead on the other side are talking to them, as already illustrated, deny, finally, every fundamental of the Christian faith.

The cross is at best but martyrdom, the Son of God in His highest attainment simply a psychic, preternatural as admitted, but in no way a specific and unique redeemer of the souls of men. Since, as they believe, communication comes from the other side of the grave, from the dead themselves; since the dead give full description of the country in which they dwell as in " Raymond," and in some degree the course of coming events, there is no need of the Bible. The Bible is, therefore, logically set aside; and when that goes, Christianity, as set forth in the Bible, goes. It is not long after that for " new " revelations and " vital " messages.

God warns His own people not to seek to the dead; as it is written:

" When thou (the nation of Israel) art come into the land which the Lord thy God giveth thee; thou shalt not learn to do after the abomination of those nations.

" There shall not be found among you any one that useth divination, or an observer of times, or an enchanter, or a witch,

" Or a charmer, or a consulter with familiar spirits, or a wizard, or a necromancer. (A necromancer is a medium, or one who purports to give messages from the dead.   The word comes from 'nekros,' a corpse, and 'manteia,' to divine.)

"For all that do these things are an abomination unto the Lord" (Deuteronomy 18: 9–13).

"And the soul that turneth after such as have familiar spirits, and after wizards, to go a whoring after them, I . . . will cut him off from among his people" (Leviticus 20: 6).

What God forbids is not of God, but of Satan.

The demonstration of that is found in the words of the demoniac of Gadara.

This is what he said:

"What have I to do with thee, Jesus, thou Son of God most high?"

This was the confession of the spirits in the man.

They confessed they had no part nor lot with the Son of God.

They were under the bonds of Satanic power.

They belonged to the region of the pit and not to the plane of Heaven.

They knew Jesus as the Son of God, but it was a knowledge that did not avail them.

They believe in the unity of God and know this unity is concretely manifested in the Son of God, in whom dwelleth all the fullness of the godhead bodily; but it makes them tremble; as it is written:

"The devils (demons) also believe and tremble."

Our Lord's own attitude toward demons and unclean spirits of every sort in casting them out and rebuking their assaults bears witness not only of the character of the demons, of all who seek to thrust themselves into this world from the unseen, but His judgment of them.

Demons and wandering spirits are wholly of Satan.

So markedly true is this that He would not allow them to testify in His behalf.

Mark tells us of a man possessed by an unclean spirit, a demon who cried out and said:

" Let us alone (they are always in companies or pairs when possible), what have we to do with thee, thou Jesus of Nazareth? art thou come to destroy us? I know thee who thou art, the Holy One of God."

They knew what the nation of Israel did not know, failed to apprehend, even with the light of their own Scriptures, that Jesus of Nazareth was the Holy One of Israel.

But, we are told, the Lord " rebuked him," and bade him come out.

Again it is written and in the same connection:

" He cast out many devils (demons) and suffered not the devils (demons) to speak, because they knew him."

" He suffered them not to speak: for they knew that he was Christ."

It is an immense warning that though a spiritist should come to you and tell you he believed in Jesus Christ, accepted Him as the Son of God and believed in His redemption, or sought under the influence of a spirit to testify in His behalf, you should reject his confession and refuse to accept his testimony.

The apostles took this attitude.

When a young woman possessed with or under the " control " of a wandering spirit followed Paul and Silas in the streets of Philippi and cried out that they were the servants of the Most High God who showed unto the people the way of salvation, Paul commanded him to come out of her.

The foresight and wisdom of God in all this is manifest.

The Devil has transformed himself into an angel of light, and his ministers into ministers of righteousness.

This is the testimony and warning of Holy Scripture.

They speak in the name of Christ, deceive in the name of Christ.

At first they lead the soul on in the simple way of faith, not disturbing it. Presently they begin to lead more and more to the contemplation of Christ in His earthly life, His spotless manhood and deeds of healing. Little by little they suggest doubts about His death as of sacrificial value. Farther and farther away do they lead from the cross. Step by step doubts are raised about the correctness of the text; after that it is not long before the Christ of God as Redeemer and Saviour is set aside.

Always the Devil is willing you shall believe in an ethical, but never in a sacrificial Christ.

Always he is willing you shall do good works and cast the hope of your hereafter on the merit of your own character of righteousness. It is not strange then that testimony after testimony of a certain class of spiritists is to the sweetness and light of the Son of God; but if you follow them with the keen intent of discovering their motive you will find them by and by regretting that this beautiful soul of Christ and all His wonderful life have been so misinterpreted (?) and overloaded with a theology foreign to His intent.

That is their scheme and they never fail to round up at that.

They speak and testify exactly like some modern ministers of Christ (?) in the pulpit.

Since Christ and His apostles repudiated Spiritism, refused to receive testimony from it, cast out the demons and the spirits that sought to speak in His name; since the Word of God in unqualified terms forbids the follower of God to have aught to do with spirits, under no circumstance, or by any means whatsoever, to seek communication from the dead, then the professed Christian who to-day meddles in any fashion with these things violates the express command of God and throws himself open to His sudden swift, providential judgment as in the case of Saul, whom He slew because he had turned away from the Word of God and inquired of the dead.

XIV

THERE NEVER WAS A TIME WHEN CHRISTIANS MORE NEEDED TO BE ON GUARD THAN NOW

THE world is growing better. That is the watchword. Everybody says it.

It is repeated in ever varying phrase. It is the utterance of the public speaker and in its attempted demonstration fills the literature of the hour.

There is a higher tone in morals, that is the affirmation; and nothing, it is said, more positively proves it than the fact this great nation has voluntarily turned from the drink habit and determined the coming generation shall, not only not be tempted by alcohol, but shall know nothing of its poison and power of woe.

The churches are everywhere entering into social work.

They have come out upon broader and more practical planes.

They have ceased to live up in heavenly places and drawn nearer to the world in which they dwell every day.

They have gotten rid of the disturbing idea that

Christ is coming back personally and visibly to this world.

They are not bothering themselves with thoughts about a golden city in Heaven, they are wholly taken up with cities down here that are altogether far from golden.

Everywhere men in the pulpits are talking grandiloquently of the new world movement for upbuilding it and setting it in the plane of righteousness.

The " principles of Christ " are to be applied in every department of world activity.

God is the Father of all men and all men should know it.

All men are brothers, partakers of a common divinity and ought to be brought together that they may make manifest the divinity of love and graciousness naturally in them.

The supreme article of faith is the golden rule.

It should be insisted upon as the center article of faith because it is the one credal expression in which all can join without dissent, Jew and Gentile, Unitarian and Trinitarian, Idolater and Materialist.   The practice of the golden rule, it is said, will soften the asperities of life and make common fellowship easier.

The sermon on the mount has precedence of the sermon from the cross.

The sermon on the mount tells men how they ought to live, the sermon from the cross tells men how Christ died for men because they are not able to live as they ought.

The sermon on the mount is more pleasing and acceptable to all than the sermon from the cross; for the sermon there is preached in the crimson of the blood which protests against the works of self-righteousness and substitutes the righteousness of God.

The concentrated effort of the world and the Church now is to make the earth a decent and safe place to live in.

The world and the Church have made common cause for this objective.

Theology has fallen into desuetude and in many respects has become not only innocuous, but thoroughly obnoxious.

The name of Christ was never so sounded forth.

His humanity is exalted by both the Church and the world.

The Church and the world sing together about His goodness.

The Church and the world both agree He came into the world to lay down the principles of a social reform that will abolish old abuses and bring in a millennium of mutual understanding among peoples so that speedily war will be like a forgotten nightmare.

Never were the Church and the world in such happy concord.

All faiths and no faiths can sit together in blissful unity and listen to the eulogies of the man Christ Jesus and rejoice that such a being ever came to earth to show men the way of peace and righteousness.

The man who has any particular conviction concerning doctrine and insists on testifying about it is put in the background with a pleasant forgiveness or gentle toleration of his enervating partizanship and narrowness; while the man who has no doctrine and no conviction save the conviction that there should be no doctrine finds the higher seat and is asked to lead the meeting in the name of that Christ who said if any man should do His will he should know of the doctrine, and soon makes it manifest that he has advanced far beyond Paul who said the preacher should hold fast the form of sound words, meaning thereby sound doctrine.

Back of all this is a pleased Devil and his cohorts.

The more the world becomes pure and clean on a natural basis; the more the ethical standard is exalted; the more Christ is named as a good man, even a divine man and leader of others up the highway of innate righteousness, the more it will please him who in his magistral determination to make this world at last his own, and that with the help of the professing Church, counts these things but as the elements of success in his ever-unfolding Satanic plan.

It is time for Christians taught of God and who believe the Bible, the written Word, is the revelation of His mind and will, to be on guard, not to allow themselves to be deceived with catch words and sounding phrases, and to remember that such an one as Paul the Apostle said (at the risk of being labelled a back number and indicated as living in a circumscribed area whose lines he had ploughed around himself by sticking too close to words and mere forms of thought) if any one, even were he an angel from Heaven, should preach any other Gospel than what he preached, of a Christ who " gave himself for our sins, that he might deliver us from this present evil world, according to the will of God and our Father," he should be accursed at the Coming of Christ.

These are the days of peril of which the Apostle has warned the Church.

The underworld of demons and the world of wandering spirits are both greatly excited.

When our Lord came the first time these worlds were greatly excited.   They were all agog.

Satan flung himself on every path the Son of God sought to tread.

He tempted Him on the mount with the vision of world rulership He might have without going to the cross.

The Devil failed.

Having failed with Christ the Head he has tempted the Church, the professing Body.

He has succeeded in a great degree.

Winning the world for Christ and setting up His

kingdom while He is away, ruling over the world and swaying it like a regency in His name, has a glamour about it, and all the organs at full octave are already playing the triumphal march.

All the spirit world is moved with the wisdom of the fallen angel.

The spirits of the dark zone are coming forth in a spiritistic revival.

A wave of spiritism is sweeping the whole earth.

Raymond says fifty per cent. of the world will soon be spiritistic.

Should it increase and the faith of the true Christ be in a large measure swept out of the great cities, then all the legislation enacted and all the efforts made by the righteous to stem the tide would be futile and the community would be submerged beneath an overflow of the sewerage of immorality and the abomination of unbelief and infidelity.

The tide will deepen.

It will submerge multitudes, specially in the great cities where contact is closer and contagion quicker.

There will be great signs and wonders; so great that if it were possible they should deceive the very elect, that bit of salt God always reserves to Himself in the earth against the day of corruption.

The Lord has given full warning.

He has said:

" Behold, I have told you before."

It will be the mighty and final effort of Satan to

capture the world and enthrone himself in the light of progress and education as its easily accepted prince and potentate.

It is witness he is preparing the way for the revelation of the super-man, the occult man, the man concerning whom all unconsciously the world has been getting ready, talking about him and vizualizing him in its plays, its dramas, spectacles and literature.

It is a common feeling, the current of it is running more strongly and universally than many dream, that man is divine and has in him powers never yet developed, powers that are akin to deity.

The study of man has never been as universal and analytical. He has taken himself apart anatomically. He has set himself apart as skin man, flesh man, bone man, muscle man, nerve man, and now with insistent intensity he is seeking to analyze himself in his soul substance and its essential relation to the unseen. He who is by nature utterly materialistic and antagonistic to everything that is spiritual is searching to find the unseen and spiritistic man that is either himself or the product of a combination of selves. He is interested not in spiritual, but spiritistic things; and between the two there is a measureless distance. That which is spiritual has in it the substance and character of the Holy Spirit of God. That which is spiritistic, in itself has no relation to God, and in essence is changelessly antagonistic.

The belief is that some day out of all this study and analysis, out of all this education and culture of the psychic there will rise a particular specimen of super-man who will point the way to the great things of which humanity is capable.

The bonds will be thrown off and man will be seen as the mental power in the earth sphere, able, presently, to control its forces, not by mere mechanics, but by the exercise of an unleashed will.

Too long this will has been dormant, subservient, ready to accept its apparent limitations.

Levitation, hypnotism, telepathy, the principles underlying wireless telephony, the relation of mind to mind, the sudden concentration of all minds in one mind and will that flings a crowd as a unit of force, all hint and suggest an outreach of terrible power yet coming to the hand of man.

The phrase, " the Coming Man," is not infrequently on the lips of men.

Whenever some great vision of what man ought to do is set up and is not yet realizable, men say, " wait till the Coming Man arrives."

So we hear of the " new man," and the " new woman."

" The Coming Man! "

The Word of God has a long while ago given the portrait of Him.

Between fifty and sixty titles are accorded Him in Holy Scripture.

The Prophet Ezekiel announces Him as one who will boldly say, " I am God."

Isaiah represents him as saying:

" I will be like the Most High."

Paul tells us He will show Himself as God.

He will be the representative of that spirit of self-deification that is now operating in man.

Spiritism is the impulse behind it, and Spiritism is but the agency in the hands of that great fallen angel who still retains his title as the prince and god of this world and of long date is determined to fulfill and function it.

It is the prelude of the hour that will begin with a false peace, a false prosperity, the world acclaiming a false Christ, seeing in this bland and winning personage as he will first reveal himself, the Coming Man for whom the world has long waited as the realization and glory of man's best powers, and a millennium brought in by education, self-culture and self-development.   An hour that will end with the mask torn from the face of the super-man and the wild orgie of the damned loosed from their prison pit and the submerging tide of the revolted spirits of the spirit zone, till the earth shall rock like a ship in the storm, and all the unbound powers of hell shall bring in that time of tribulation such as the Son of God says the world never saw and never will see again—the wild upheaval of all that is against God and His Christ till the shadow of the old eclipse and chaos, moral and physical, seems to be upon the quivering earth as it staggers like a drunken man in the path of its orbit.

It is Satan's wild desperate fling against God's Christ in the determination to put his own son on the throne of the world and hold it through him.

It will fail, of course.

God's Son, the true Super-man, will arise from His borrowed throne in Heaven and come forth to smite this partnership of man and Devil and bring in the kingdom of everlasting righteousness and truth.

Spiritism, therefore, while it bears witness of the coming of Satan's hour, bears witness also of the Coming of Christ as the true King and God of this world.

Every accent of unbelief, all the subtleties of spirit invasion and all the apparent triumph of Satanic power are but the witnesses that the day will break at last and the radiant face of the kingly Christ shall be seen before whom a liberated world will bow in adoration and proclaim His praise.

Since it is true according to the Word of God that before our Lord appears in His glory He will come as a bridegroom comes for his bride; since it is true He will come to take the true and regenerated Church to Himself that she may be above the wild storm that will sweep the earth in the short reign of Satan's super-man; as it is true there is not a single predicted event between us and that moment when He will shout the Church up to Himself, then the call to the Church to be ready is more insistent now than ever.

Long ago He said:

" Watch ye therefore: for ye know not when the master of the house cometh, at even, or at midnight, or at the cock-crowing, or in the morning:

" Lest coming suddenly he find you sleeping.

" And what I say unto you I say unto all, Watch."

He did not come at even, the midnight is on us, here and there are sounds of the cock-crowing.

The Cock-crowing!

I have heard it in the mountain country. Far up on the mountain side chanticleer announced the midnight passing and the morning hour at hand; then in the valley far below an answering cry took up the midnight challenge, and farther away another, and yet another till the whole air was full of cock-crowing and the thin grey morning began to touch the edge of midnight darkness.

And what is cock-crowing but the fulfillment of divine prophecy, the answering signs of the times which tell us He is near? signs in the professing Church, in the nations of the Roman earth, signs amid blind and unbelieving Judah, Jerusalem delivered, the symbolic Euphrates drying up, the shadow of Antichrist growing deeper as we turn our eyes to the East and everywhere this quiver of the unseen world, of imprisoned demons and wan-

dering spirits getting ready to greet him and give
him the all hail.

Midnight, we say, is always darkest before the
dawning.

Well may we watch in this darkness, this spiritual midnight, listen to the cock-crowing as here
and there it is sounding, wait and be ready for the
morning.